Study Guide

M000272963

Criminal Justice in Action

SIXTH EDITION

Larry K. Gaines
California State University
San Bernardino

Roger LeRoy Miller
Institute for University Studies
Arlington, Texas

Prepared by

Todd Scott
Schoolcraft College

WADSWORTH
CENGAGE Learning™

Australia • Brazil • Japan • Korea • Mexico • Singapore • Spain • United Kingdom • United States

WADSWORTH
CENGAGE Learning

For product information and technology assistance, contact us at **Cengage Learning Customer & Sales Support, 1-800-354-9706**

For permission to use material from this text or product, submit all requests online at **www.cengage.com/permissions** Further permissions questions can be emailed to **permissionrequest@cengage.com**

ISBN-13: 978-0-495-81105-3
ISBN-10: 0-495-81105-X

Wadsworth
20 Davis Drive
Belmont, CA 94002-3098
USA

Cengage Learning is a leading provider of customized learning solutions with office locations around the globe, including Singapore, the United Kingdom, Australia, Mexico, Brazil, and Japan. Locate your local office at: **www.cengage.com/global**

Cengage Learning products are represented in Canada by Nelson Education, Ltd.

To learn more about Wadsworth, visit **www.cengage.com/wadsworth**

Purchase any of our products at your local college store or at our preferred online store **www.ichapters.com**

Printed in the United States of America
1 2 3 4 5 6 7 13 12 11 10 09

TABLE OF CONTENTS

CHAPTER 1

CRIMINAL JUSTICE TODAY

OUTLINE

- What is Crime?
- The Criminal Justice System
- Values of the Criminal Justice System
- Criminal Justice Today
- Criminal Justice in Action—Gun Control versus Gun Rights

Learning Objectives

After reading this chapter, you should be able to:

LO1: Describe the two most common models of how society determines which acts are criminal.
LO2: Define "crime" and identify the different types of crime.
LO3: Outline the three levels of law enforcement.
LO4: List the essential elements of the correctional system.
LO5: Explain the difference between the formal and informal criminal justice processes.
LO6: Describe the layers of the "wedding cake" model.
LO7: Contrast the crime control and due process models.
LO8: List the major issues in criminal justice today.

Chapter Outline

I. What is Crime?
    a. Crime – an act that violates criminal law and is punishable by criminal sanctions
  A. The Consensus Model
    a. Majority of citizens in a society share the same values and beliefs. Criminal acts are acts that conflict with these beliefs
  B. The Conflict Model
    a. Content of criminal law is determined by the groups that hold economic, political, and social power in a community
  C. An Integrated Definition of Crime
    a. Punishable under criminal law
    b. Considered an offense against society
    c. Punishable by statutorily determined sanctions
    d. Deviance – behavior that is considered to go against the norms established by society
  D. Types of Crime
    1. Violent Crime
      a. Murder
        i. Unlawful killing
      b. Sexual assault/Rape
        i. Forced or coerced sexual intercourse
      c. Assault
        i. Threat or attempt to do violence to another person that causes that person to fear immediate physical harm
      d. Battery
        i. The act of physically contacting another person with the intent to do harm

2

      e. Robbery
         i. Taking property from another person through force, threat of force, or intimidation
   2. Property Crime
      a. Larceny/theft
         i. Taking property from another person without the use of force
      b. Burglary
         i. Breaking into or entering a structure without permission for the purpose of committing a crime
      c. Motor vehicle theft
      d. Arson
   3. Public Order Crime
      a. Behavior that has been labeled criminal because it is contrary to shared social values, customs, and norms
         i. Also called victimless
         ii. Public drunkenness, gambling, prostitution
   4. White-collar Crime
         i. Embezzlement
         ii. Mail and wire fraud
         iii. Credit card and check fraud
         iv. Insurance fraud
         v. Securities fraud
         vi. Bribery
         vii. Consumer fraud
         viii. Tax evasion
   5. Organized Crime
         i. Conspiratorial relationship
         ii. Hierarchical structure
   6. High-Tech Crime
      a. Cyber crime
         i. Against persons: obscenity and pornography, cyberstalking, cyber harassment
         ii. Against property: Hacking, cracking, piracy, viruses
         iii. Against the government: cyberterrorism
II. The Criminal Justice System
      a. The interlocking network of law enforcement agencies, courts, and corrections institutions designed to enforce criminal laws and protect society from criminal behavior
  A. The Purpose of the Criminal Justice System
   1. Controlling and Preventing Crime
   2. Maintaining Justice
  B. The Structure of the Criminal Justice System
      a. The Concept of Federalism
         i. Government powers are shared by the federal government and the states

3

1. Law Enforcement
   a. Local Law Enforcement
   b. State Law Enforcement
   c. Federal Law Enforcement
2. The Courts
   a. Dual court system:
      i. State courts: trial courts, courts of appeal, state supreme courts.
      ii. Federal courts: district courts, circuit courts of appeals, United States Supreme Court
   b. Courtroom work group: judges, prosecutors, defense attorneys
3. Corrections
   a. Probation
   b. Incarceration
      i. Prisons
      ii. Jails
   c. Community-Based Corrections
C. The Criminal Justice Process
   1. The Assembly Line
   2. The Formal Criminal Justice Process
   3. The Informal Criminal Justice Process
      i. Discretion – the ability of individuals in the criminal justice system to make operational decisions based on personal judgment instead of formal rules or official information
      a. Discretionary Basics
         i. Police
            01. Enforce laws
            02. Investigate crimes
            03. Search people and buildings
            04. Arrest or detain people
         ii. Prosecutors
            01. File charges against suspects
            02. Drop cases
            03. Reduce charges
         iii. Judges
            01. Set conditions for pre-trial release
            02. Accept pleas
            03. Dismiss charges
            04. Impose sentences
         iv. Corrections Officials
            01. Assign convicts to institutions
            02. Punish misbehaving prisoners
            03. Reward prisoners who behave well
      b. Discretionary Values
      c. The "Wedding Cake" Model of Criminal Justice
         i. Celebrated cases
         ii. Serious or high-profile felonies

4

        iii. Less serious felonies
        iv. Misdemeanors
III. Values of the Criminal Justice System
    A. Crime Control and Due Process: To Punish or Protect?
            i.   Civil rights – personal rights and protections guaranteed by the Constitution, particularly the Bill of Rights
        1. The Crime Control Model
            i.   Places primary emphasis on the right of society to be protected from crime and violent criminals
        a. Assembly-line justice
        b. Goals:
            i.   Deter crime
            ii. Protect citizens from crime
            iii. Incapacitate criminals
            iv. Provide quick and efficient justice
        c. Means to These Goals
            i.   Promote discretion and eliminate bureaucracy
            ii. Make it easier for police to arrest criminals
            iii. Reduce restrictions on proving guilt at trial
        2. The Due Process Model
            i.   Places primary emphasis on the right of the individual to be protected from the power of the government
        a. Justice as an obstacle course
        b. Goals
            i.   Protect the individual against the immense power of the state
            ii. Rehabilitate those convicted of crime
        c. Means to the Goals
            i.   Limit state power and uphold constitutional rights
    B. Which Model Prevails Today?
        1. The pendulum swings
        2. Responding to terrorism
IV. Criminal Justice Today
    A. Violent Crime: The Bottom Line
        1. Reality check
           a. Fear and violent crime
        2. Gun Sales and Gun Control
           a. Gun control – efforts by a government to regulate or control the sale of guns
        3. The Illegal Drugs Problem
           a. Drug – any substance that modified biological, psychological, or social behavior
           b. Psychoactive drugs – chemicals that affect the brain, causing changes in emotions, perceptions, and behavior
           c. Drug Use in the United States
              i.   National Survey on Drug Use and Health
                 01. National Institute on Drug Abuse

B. Law Enforcement in the United States: Challenging Success
    1. The Scourge of Street Gangs
       a. Street gang – a group of people, usually three or more, who share a common identity and engage in illegal activities
    2. DNA Profiling
    3. Homeland Security
       i. A concerted national effort to prevent terrorist attacks within the U.S. and reduce the country's vulnerability to terrorism
       a. Terrorism – the use or threat of violence to achieve political objectives
C. Crime and Punishment
    3. The Growing Prison Population
    4. Diversion and Execution
V. Criminal Justice in Action—Gun Control versus Gun Rights

Key Terms

assault (pg. 8)
battery (pg. 8)
burglary (pg. 8)
civil rights (pg. 20)
conflict model (pg. 7)
consensus model (pg. 6)
crime (pg. 5)
crime control model (pg. 20)
criminal justice system (pg. 10)
deviance (pg. 7)
discretion (pg. 17)
due process model (pg. 20)
drug (pg. 24)
federalism (pg. 11)
gun control (pg. 24)
high-tech crime (pg. 8)
homeland security (pg. 27)
larceny (p. 8)
murder (pg. 8)
organized crime (pg. 9)
psychoactive drugs (pg. 24)
public order crime (pg. 8)
robbery (pg. 8)
sexual assault (pg. 8)
street gang (pg. 25)
terrorism (pg. 27)
wedding cake model (pg. 18)
white collar crime (pg.9)

Special Projects

1. Attend a court proceeding at your local/district court. What kind of activity did you observe? Were any of the concepts or key terms from the chapter a part of the proceedings? What did you learn? Prepare a hypothetical in-class report on your visit. Include the details of at least one court action in your report.

2. Identify a technological advancement that has been beneficial to law enforcement in the past five years. Use the Internet (popular media) to conduct your research. Identify the technology and outline all of the major benefits.

3. Using popular media, research a white collar crime. Identify the crime and outline the case. What was the outcome of the case? Identify any victims. Were there other criminal cases associated with the crime?

Practice Test

True-False

__F__ 1.   A crime is a wrong against an individual.

__F__ 2.   The consensus model asserts that laws are determined by the groups that hold economic or political power.

__F__ 3.   In the criminal justice field there is universal consensus on what constitutes a crime.

__T__ 4.   The top layer of the wedding cake model represents idealized justice.

__T__ 5.   Assault and battery are two separate acts.

__T__ 6.   Public order crime is often referred to as "victimless crime."

__T__ 7.   The most common form of criminal activity is property crime.

__F__ 8.   Discretion is an important part of the formal criminal justice system.

__F__ 9.   The prison population has remained fairly stable for the last decade.

__F__ 10.   The due process model sees justice as an assembly-line.

Multiple Choice

1. The ability of individuals in the criminal justice system to make operational decisions based on personal judgment instead of formal rules or official information is
    a. bias.
    b. prejudicial.
    c. precedent.
    d. discretion.

2. In which layer of the wedding cake model of justice are misdemeanors located?
    a. First layer
    b. Second layer
    c. Third layer
    d. Fourth layer

3. Society places the burden of controlling and preventing crime on all of the following EXCEPT
    a. law enforcement.
    b. corrections.
    c. victims.
    d. courts.

4. The wedding cake model of the criminal justice system
    a. shows how disjointed the system really is.
    b. focuses only on celebrity cases.
    c. allows crime to go unchecked.
    d. is useful for understanding how much system energy is spent on different tiers of crime.

5. Local law enforcement has the primary responsibility of
    a. patrolling interstate highways.
    b. investigating federal law violations.
    c. pursuing international fugitives.
    d. taking care of the "nuts and bolts" of police work.

6. "Organized crime" refers to
    a. illegal acts by illegal organizations.
    b. behavior that has been labeled criminal because it is contrary to shared social values.
    c. the "Mafia."
    d. illegal acts by employees of legitimate businesses.

7. Approximately how many people are killed in the United States by gunfire each year?
    a. 30,000
    b. 60,000
    c. 90,000
    d. 110,000

8. The most common correctional system treatment is
    a. probation.
    b. incarceration in jail.
    c. incarceration in prison.
    d. community corrections.

9. Which of the following is NOT considered a public order crime?
    a. Prostitution
    b. Gambling
    c. Illicit drug use
    d. Arson

10. All of the following are considered white collar crimes EXCEPT
    a. embezzlement.
    b. extortion.
    c. bribery.
    d. tax invasion.

11. The conflict model asserts that
    a. society can agree on shared morals.
    b. determination of the law is made by majority of the people.
    c. crimes are offenses against the whole society.
    d. laws are designed to enforce shared norms.

12. Violent crimes include all of the following EXCEPT
    a. murder.
    b. sexual assault.
    c. burglary.
    d. robbery

13. Which of the following statements regarding deviance is true?
    a. Deviance is a subjective concept
    b. Society agrees on which behaviors are considered deviant
    c. All deviant behaviors are criminal
    d. All crimes are considered deviant behavior

14. The types of cyber crime, as identified in the text, include all of the following EXCEPT
    a. spamming.
    b. hacking/cracking.
    c. cyberstalking.
    d. cyber fraud.

15. Which of the following is NOT one of the goals of the criminal justice system?
    a. Rehabilitate offenders
    b. Prevent crime
    c. Control crime
    d. Provide and maintain justice

16. The concept that governance is shared by federal and state government is
    a. separation of powers.
    b. bureaucracy.
    c. federalism.
    d. democracy.

17. In general, what level of law enforcement do fire marshals and fish and game wardens occupy?
    a. Municipal
    b. County
    c. State
    d. Federal

18. Which of the following facilities is most likely to hold pretrial detainees and persons convicted of minor offenses?
    a. Prisons
    b. Jails
    c. Detention centers
    d. Day reporting centers

19. Which layer of the wedding cake includes ordinary felony cases?
    a. First
    b. Second
    c. Third
    d. Fourth

20. Biometrics is a burgeoning technology that can assist law enforcement with the identification of missing persons through
    a. DNA profiling.
    b. facial recognition systems.
    c. blood analysis.
    d. enhanced dental identification.

21. The due process model
   a. incarcerates offenders.
   b. focuses on efficiency.
   c. assures constitutional rights of all accused persons.
   d. operates on the presumption of guilt.

22. The crime control model
   a. rehabilitates offenders.
   b. incarcerates criminals.
   c. limits police discretion.
   d. protects individuals from the power of the state.

23. DNA profiling provides law enforcement with the ability to identify a suspect by
   a. scanning an individual's iris.
   b. examining an individual's bodily fluid.
   c. using a voice stress analyzer.
   d. typing an individual's fingerprint.

24. The police have discretion to
   a. enforce laws.
   b. bring offenders to trial.
   c. dismiss charges against offenders.
   d. sentence juvenile offenders.

25. Over the past decade, violent crime rates
   a. have remained stable.
   b. have dramatically increased.
   c. have slowly increased.
   d. have declined.

Fill in the Blank

1. A _____crime_____ is punishable by statutorily determined sanctions that bring about the loss of personal freedom or life.

2. Historically, societies have always outlawed activities that are considered contrary to _____morals_____ and public values.

3. The _____consensus_____ model asserts that the majority of citizens in a society share the same values and beliefs. Criminal acts that conflict with this idea are deemed harmful to society.

11

4. The ___conflict___ model asserts that the content of criminal law is determined by the groups that hold economic, political, and social power in a community.

5. Murder, robbery, sexual assault, and assault and battery are all categorized as ___violent___ crimes.

6. Behavior is said to be ___deviant___ if it goes against the norms established by society.

7. The unlawful killing of a human being is ___murder___.

8. Sexual ___assault___ is coerced action of another that is sexual in nature.

9. When one person physically attacks another, it is a ___battery___.

10. The taking of cash or other goods from a person by force or fear is ___robbery___.

11. Stealing property without the use of force is ___theft/larceny___.

12. Unlawful entry into a structure to commit another crime is ___burglary___.

13. The decision points in the criminal justice system are often called ___discretion___.

14. A synonym for public order crime is ___victimless___ crime.

15. Nonviolent crimes committed by business entities or individuals to gain a personal or business advantage are known as ___white collar___ crime.

16. Illegal acts by illegal organizations are called ___organized___ crime.

17. Hacking, cracking, theft of proprietary data, and cyber fraud are examples of ___cyber___ crime.

18. The interlocking network of law enforcement agencies, courts, and correctional institutions designed to enforce criminal laws and protect society from criminal behavior is formally known as the ___Criminal Justice System___.

19. Local law enforcement is concentrated at the ___municipal___ level of government.

20. _Federalism_ means that government powers are shared by the national (federal) government and the states.

21. The _dual_ court system describes the two independent court systems that operate within the United States.

22. Probation and incarceration are parts of the _Corrections_ system.

23. Typically _jails_ hold pretrial detainees (persons awaiting trial and sentencing).

24. Other than by expiration of sentence, the most frequent release from prison is by way of _parole_.

25. The creation of programs harmful to computers, such as worms, trojan horses, and viruses is known as _malware_ production.

26. Walker's wedding cake model of criminal justice has _four_ layers.

27. The _crime control_ model asserts the right of society to be protected from crime and violent criminals.

28. The "get tough" type laws have caused _prison_ populations to rise.

29. _Diversion_ programs funnel offenders away from incarceration and into special courts that focus on rehabilitation.

30. _Terrorism_ is the use or threat of violence to achieve political objectives.

Short Essays

1. Compare and contrast the consensus models with the conflict models. Determine if they are mutually exclusive.

13

2. Define crime and explain the different types of crime.

3. Outline the three levels of law enforcement.

4. Describe the essential elements of the corrections system.

14

5. Contrast the formal and informal criminal justice processes.

6. How does the wedding cake model of the criminal justice system aid us in understanding the system? Is there a negative side to describing the system as a wedding cake?

7. Compare and contrast the crime control model with the due process model.

8. Select and discuss two of the major issues in criminal justice today.

Answer Key

True-False:
1. F, see pg. 5, LO2/5
2. F, see pg. 6, LO1
3. F, see pg. 5, LO2
4. T, see pg. 18, LO6
5. T, see pg. 8, LO2
6. T, see pg. 8, LO2
7. T, see pg. 8, LO2
8. F, see pg. 17, LO5
9. F, see pg. 28, LO8
10. F, see pg. 20, LO7

Multiple Choice:
1. d, see pg. 17, LO5
2. d, see pg. 19, LO6
3. c, see pg. 11, LO3
4. d, see pg. 19, LO6
5. d, see pg. 13, LO3
6. a, see pgs. 9-10, LO2
7. a, see pg. 24, LO7
8. a, see pg. 15, LO4
9. d, see pg. 8, LO2.
10. b, see pg. 9, LO2
11. b, see pg. 7, LO1
12. c, see pg. 8, LO2
13. a, see pg. 7, LO1
14. a, see pg. 10,LO2
15. a, see pg. 11, LO3
16. c, see pg. 11, LO3
17. c, see pg. 13, LO3
18. b, see pg. 15, LO4
19. c, see pg. 19, LO6
20. b, see pg. 27, LO8
21. c, see pg. 20, LO7
22. b, see pg. 20, LO7
23. b, see pg. 26, LO8
24. a, see pg. 17, LO5
25. d, see pg. 24, LO8

Fill in the Blank:
1. crime, see pg. 5, LO2
2. morals, see pg. 6, LO1
3. consensus, see pg. 6, LO1
4. conflict, see pg. 7, LO1
5. violent, see pg. 8, LO2
6. deviant, see pg. 7, LO1
7. murder, see pg. 8, LO2
8. sexual, see pg. 8, LO2
9. battery, see pg. 8, LO2
10. robbery, see pg. 8, LO2
11. larceny, see pg. 8, LO2.
12. burglary, see pg. 8, LO2
13. discretion, see pg. 17, LO5
14. victimless, see pg. 8, LO2
15. white collar, see pg. 9, LO2
16. organized, see pgs. 8-9, LO2
17. cyber, see pg. 10, LO2
18. criminal justice system, see pg. 10, LO3
19. municipal, see pg. 12, LO3
20. Federalism, see pg. 11, LO3
21. dual, see pg. 15, LO3
22. corrections, see pg. 15, LO4
23. Jail, see pg. 15, LO4
24. parole, see pg. 16, LO4
25. malware, see pg. 10, LO2
26. four, see pg. 19, LO6
27. crime control, see pg. 20, LO7
28. prison, see pg. 28, LO8
29. diversion, see pg. 29, LO8
30. terrorism, see pg. 27, LO8

Short Essays:
1. See pgs. 6-7, LO1
2. See pgs. 7-10, LO2
3. See pgs. 12-15, LO3
4. See pg. 15, LO4
5. See pgs. 16-17, LO5
6. See pgs. 17-18, LO6
7. See pg. 20, LO7
8. See pgs. 21-26, LO8

CHAPTER 2

CAUSES OF CRIME

OUTLINE

- Theory in Criminology
- Exploring the Causes of Crime
- Further Study: Expanding Criminology
- The Link between Drugs and Crime
- Criminology from Theory to Practice
- Criminal Justice in Action—The Link Between Violent Video Games and Crime

Learning Objectives

After reading this chapter, you should be able to:

LO1: Discuss the difference between a hypothesis and a theory in the context of criminology.

LO2: Explain why classical criminology is based on choice theory.

LO3: Contrast positivism with classical criminology.

LO4: List and describe the three theories of social structure that help explain crime.

LO5: List and briefly explain the three branches of social process theory.

LO6: Describe how life course criminology differs from the other theories addressed in this chapter.

LO7: Discuss the connection between offenders and victims of crime.

LO8: Contrast the medical model of addiction with the criminal model of addiction.

LO9: Explain the theory of the chronic offender and its importance for the criminal justice system.

Chapter Outline

I. Theory in Criminology
   a. Criminologist – a specialist in the field of crime and the causes of criminal behavior
   A. The Role of Theory
      a. Theory- an explanation of a happening or circumstance that is based on observation, experimentation, and reasoning
      b. Hypothesis – a possible explanation for an observed occurrence that can be tested by further investigation
   B. The Fallibility of Theory
      1. A Theory Presented
      2. A Theory Rejected
II. Exploring the Causes of Crime
   A. Crime and Free Will: Choice Theories of Crime
      a. Choice theory – school of criminology that holds that wrongdoers act as if they weigh the possible benefits of criminal or delinquent behavior against the expected costs of being apprehended
      1. Theories of Classical Criminology
         a. Defining Classical Criminology
            i. Caesare Beccaria, Italian legal philosopher
            ii. Jeremy Bentham, utilitarian

20

2. Positivism and Modern Rational Choice
   a. Positivism – school of the social sciences that sees criminal and delinquent behavior as the result of biological, psychological, and social forces
   b. Cesare Lombroso and positivism
   c. Rational choice theory
3. The Seduction of Crime
   a. Jack Katz, sociologist
4. Choice Theory and Public Policy
   a. Lawmakers favor harsher punishments to deter crime.

B. "Born Criminal"—Biological and Psychological Theories of Crime (Trait Theories)
   1. Genetics and Crime
      i. Behavioral Genes
      a. Twin Studies
         i. MZ twins and DZ twins
      b. Adoption Studies
   2. Hormones and Aggression
      i. Hormones – chemical substance produced in tissue and conveyed in the bloodstream, that controls certain cellular and bodily functions such as growth and reproduction
   3. The Brain and Crime (Neurophysiology)
      a. Neurotransmitter – chemical that transmits nerve impulses between nerve cells and from nerve cells to the brain
      b. Three neurotransmitters related to aggressive behavior:
         i. Serotonin
         ii. Norepinephrine
         iii. Dopamine
      c. Neurological defects
   4. Other Biological Influences
      a. Neurotoxins
   5. Psychology and Crime
      a. Freud's Psychoanalytic Theory
         i. Three parts of the human personality:
            01. Id
            02. Ego
            03. Superego
      b. Social Psychology and "Evil" behavior
         i. Focuses on human behavior in the context of how human beings relate to and influence one another
   6. Trait Theory and Public Policy
      a. Treatment and rehabilitation

C. Sociological Theories of Crime
   1. The Chicago School
      a. Park and Burgess

21

      i.   related to social structure in disorganization theory, strain theory, and cultural deviance theory

2. Social Disorganization Theory
      i.   The theory that deviant behavior is more likely in communities where social institutions such as the family, schools, and the criminal justice system fail to exert control over the population
    a. Disorganized Zones
    b. The Value of Role Models

3. Strain theory
    a. Assumption that crime is the result of frustration felt by individuals who cannot reach their financial and personal goals through legitimate means
      i.   Emile Durkheim and anomie
        01.A condition in which the individual suffers from the breakdown or absence of social norms
      ii. Robert K. Merton—pressures in the social structure
      iii. Robert Agnew—general strain theory; negative emotionality

4. Cultural Deviance theory
    a. Assumption that members of certain subcultures reject that values of the dominant culture through deviant behavior patterns
    b. Subculture – group exhibiting certain values and behavior patterns that distinguish it from the dominant culture

5. Social Structure Theory and Public Policy
    a. Government programs attack unemployment, poverty, educational opportunity, and neighborhood conditions.

D. Family, Friends and the Media: Social Processes of Crime
    a. The General Potential to Deviate
    b. The Zimbardo Experiments
    c. Social process theories – criminal behavior is the predictable result of a person's interaction with their environment

1. Learning Theory
    b. Edwin Sutherland (Differential Association)
    c. Studies of the impact of the media

2. Control Theory
    a. All individuals have the potential for criminal behavior, but are restrained by the damage such actions would do to their relationships
      i.   Wilson and Kelling's theory of "Broken Windows"

3. Labeling Theory
    a. Perceptions of criminal behavior rather than the behavior itself

4. Social Process Theory and Public Policy

E. Social Conflict Theories
    a. Criminal behavior is the result of class conflict
      i.   Focuses on power

1. Marxism vs. Capitalism
    a. Social Reality of Crime
      i. Haves and Have Nots

2. Issues of Race and Gender
3. Social Conflict Theory and Public Policy
   a. Limited impact on public policy
   b. Suggests increased employment of women and minorities in the criminal justice system

III. Further Study: Expanding Criminology
  A. Looking Back to Childhood: Life Course Theories of Crime
     a. Agnew and Cullen's Life Course Criminology
        i. Behavioral patterns developed in childhood can predict delinquent and criminal behavior later in life
     1. Self-Control Theory
        a. Gottfredson and Hirshi's Self-Control Theory
        b. A General Theory of Crime: The "continuity of crime"
     2. The Possibility of Change
        a. Life-course-persistent offenders
        b. Adolescent-limited offenders
  B. Victimology and Victims of Crime
     a. Victimology – studies why certain people are the victims of crimes and the optimal role for victims in the criminal justice system
     1. Risks of Victimization
        a. Routine Activities Theory
           i. A likely offender
           ii. A suitable target
           iii. Absence of a capable guardian
     2. Repeat Victimization
     3. The Victim-Offender Connection

IV. The Link Between Drugs and Crime
  A. The Criminology of Drug Use
     1. Theories of Drug Use
        a. Social disorganization theory
        b. Subculture theory
     2. Drugs and the "Learning Process"
        a. Learn the techniques of drug use
        b. Learn to perceive the pleasurable effects of drug use
        c. Learn to enjoy the social experience of drug use
  B. Drug Addiction and Dependency
     1. Drug Use and Drug Abuse
        a. Drug abuse – the use of drugs that results in physical or psychological problems for the user, as well as disruption of personal relationships and employment
     2. Addiction Basics
  C. The Drug-Crime Relationship
     a. More than 2/3 of jail inmates are dependent on or abuse alcohol or drugs
     1. Models of Explanation
        a. Psychopharmacological model

23

     b. Economically impulsive model

     c. Systemic model

  2. Models of Addiction

     a. Medical model – drug abuse is a mental illness and focus is on treatment and rehabilitation

     b. Criminal model – offender harms society by their actions to the same extent as other criminals and should face the same punitive sanctions

V. Criminology from Theory to Practice

  A. Criminology and the Chronic Offender

    1. Wolfgang's Chronic Offender

  B. Criminology and the Criminal Justice System

VI. Criminal Justice in Action—The Link Between Violent Video Games and Crime

Key Terms

anomie (p. 50)

biology (pg. 44)

choice theory (p. 41)

chronic offender (pg. 65)

classical criminology (pg. 41)

control theory (pg. 53)

criminal model of addiction (pg. 63)

criminologist (pg. 39)

criminology (pg. 38)

cultural deviance theory (pg. 50)

domestic abuse (pg. 38)

drug abuse (pg. 62)

genetics (pg. 44)

hormone (pg. 44)

hypothesis (pg.39)

Labeling theory (pg. 53)

Learning theory (pg. 51)

life course criminology (pg. 57)

medical model of addiction (pg. 63)

neurotransmitter (pg. 45)

positivism (pg. 42)

psychoanalytic theory (pg.46)

psychology (pg. 44)

repeat victimization (pg. 59)

self-conflict theories (pg. 54)

social disorganization theory (pg. 49)

social process theory (pg. 51)

social reality of crime (pg. 54)

strain theory (pg. 50)
subculture (pg. 50)
testosterone (pg. 45)
theory (pg. 39)
utilitarianism (pg. 41)
victimology (pg. 58)

Special Projects

1. Use the Internet to research a criminal case where a biological or psychological variable triggered criminal behavior. Identify and outline the case. How did the variable impact the court case? What was the outcome of the case?

2. What affect does bullying have on young people? Research this question and write a short summary on what you find. Do you agree with your research? Why or why not? How common is bullying today?

3. Locate the FBI's Uniform Crime Reports (UCR). The report is available on the Internet. Locate a (1) a low income community and (2) an affluent middle-income community in the report. What do the statistics tell you? Were you surprised by your research? What did you learn?

Practice Test

True-False

_____T___ 1.   Causation means that one variable is responsible for the change in another.

_____F___ 2.   The medical model of addiction treats drug abuse as a criminal behavior eligible for criminal punishment.

_____T___ 3.   Pain and pleasure are the foundation of utilitarianism.

_____T___ 4.   The concept "seduction of crime" is an elaboration on rational choice theory.

_____T___ 5.   Trait theories suggest that biological or psychological variables can trigger criminal behavior under specific conditions.

_____T___ 6.   Post-partum psychosis has been used to justify aggression.

25

_T_ 7.   When the id, the ego, and the supergo fall into disorder, antisocial urges may develop and force the individual to commit crime.

_T_ 8.   The criminal model of addiction holds that drug offenders harm society in the same manner as all other criminals and as such, there should be no distinction in their punishment.

_F_ 9.   Social disorganization theory holds that crime is largely a product of a poorly organized social welfare system.

_T_ 10. Strain theory has its roots in the concept of *anomie*.

_F_ 11. Members of a subculture often assimilate with the larger dominant culture and they become indistinguishable from this larger dominant group.

_T_ 12. Edwin Sutherland's learning theory suggests that criminal activity is a learned behavior.

_F_ 13. Labeling theory is a social conflict theory.

_T_ 14. Social conflict theory focuses on power distributions.

_T_ 15. The social reality of crime is that the powerful get to make the rules.

_T_ 16. Bullying and lying are important variables in life course criminology.

_T_ 17. Heavy drinkers are at greater risk of being assaulted when they are intoxicated versus when sober.

_F_ 18. System revictimization refers to the propensity for certain people to be victimized more than others.

Multiple Choice

1. A hypothesis is a possible explanation for an observed reasoned occurrence that can be
    a. reasoned.
    b. explained.
    c. changed.
    d. tested.

2. A theory would be based on all of the following EXCEPT
      a. instinct.
      b. observation.
      c. experimentation.
      d. reasoning.

3. For the positivist, behavior is determined by all of the following EXCEPT
      a. by spiritual forces.
      b. by psychological forces.
      c. by social forces.
      d. by biological forces.

4. Twin studies
      a. help determine the relationship between genes and behavior.
      b. must be conducted in hospital settings.
      c. are a statistical control for police intervention.
      d. cannot be random among fraternal twins.

5. According to Freud, which part of the personality determines right and wrong?
      a. Id
      b. Ego
      c. Superego
      d. Intuition

6. The Chicago School showed a correlation between crime and
      a. ethnicity.
      b. age.
      c. substance abuse.
      d. general neighborhood conditions.

7. Which model holds that drug abusers endanger society and as such should be treated like criminals?
      a. Medical model of addiction
      b. Criminal model of addiction
      c. Law enforcement model of addiction
      d. Treatment model of addiction

8. Social process theories include all of the following EXCEPT
      a. learning theory.
      b. control theory.
      c. labeling theory.
      d. strain theory.

9. Control theory holds that although we all have the potential to commit crimes, most of us are dissuaded from doing so because we care about
   a. being officially being labeled as a criminal in the criminal justice system.
   b. the opinions of our family and peers.
   c. our social stature.
   d. our religious values.

10. Individuals who believe that crime is primarily explained through the power or ruling class subscribe to
   a. social conflict theories.
   b. social structure theories.
   c. social process theories.
   d. social composition theories.

11. The Classical school of criminology holds that individuals' act based upon
   a. free will.
   b. low intelligence.
   c. antisocial personality disorder.
   d. low self-control.

12. Who published the essays on *Crime and Punishment*?
   a. Beccaria
   b. Bentham
   c. Wolfgang
   d. Lombroso

13. The scientific study of victims did not begin until
   a. after the civil war.
   b. after World War I.
   c. after World War II.
   d. after the Vietnam War.

14. Social conflict theory includes
   a. Marxism notions.
   b. issues of neighborhood disorganization.
   c. a discussion of strain and anomie.
   d. labeling theory.

15. Victimology studies
   a. offenders and what drives them to crime.
   b. why certain people become victims.
   c. the psychology of crime.
   d. the affect of victimless crime on society.

28

16. Which one is NOT associated with choice theory?
    a. The death penalty is a deterrent
    b. Mandatory sentencing can be a powerful control
    c. Penalties add another variable to the decision process
    d. Sanctions are considered to have little or no deterrent effect

17. Biochemical explanations of misbehavior have included all of the following EXCEPT
    a. testosterone.
    b. postpartum psychosis.
    c. junk food or the "Twinkie" defense.
    d. antisocial personality disorder.

18. The superego
    a. is almost synonymous with conscience.
    b. controls sexual urges.
    c. controls behavior that leads to the fulfillment of the id.
    d. controls violent impulses.

19. Sampson and Laub suggested that some offenders cease committing crimes when they reach adulthood, these offenders are referred to as
    a. life-course persistent offenders.
    b. juvenile delinquents.
    c. adolescent-limited offenders.
    d. the chronic six percent.

20. Who developed the concept of anomie?
    a. Robert Merton
    b. Robert Agnew
    c. Thomas Bennett
    d. Emile Durkheim

21. Wolfgang's research on chronic offenders found that
    a. a chronic three percent of offenders commit crime.
    b. a chronic six percent of offenders commit crime.
    c. a chronic nine percent of offenders commit crime.
    d. a chronic twelve percent of offenders commit crime.

22. Social structure theorists believe that the best way to prevent criminal offending is to
    a. prevent juvenile offenders from being labeled.
    b. increase criminal sanctions to create deterrence.
    c. create neighborhood programs and spur revitalization.
    d. provide treatment for offenders.

29

23. The hypothesis that society creates crime and criminals by labeling certain behavior and certain people as deviant is
      a. control theory.
      b. labeling theory.
      c. prodigy theory.
      d. utilitarian theory.

24. All of the following are elements of routine activity theory EXCEPT
      a. a motivated offender.
      b. a suitable target.
      c. community disorganization.
      d. absence of a capable guardian.

25. Which groups are victimized more frequently than others?
      a. Young males
      b. Mentally challenged
      c. Senior citizens
      d. Young girls

Fill in the Blank

1. When two variables tend to vary together, they are said to have a __Correlation__

2. In the United States, the general presumption in criminal law has been that behavior is a consequence of __free will__.

3. An updated version of classical theory is __rational choice__ theory.

4. Biological theories focus on the effect that __genes__ have on crime.

5. Criminal activity in males has been linked to the hormone __testosterone__.

6. __Dopamine__ regulates perceptions of pleasure and reward.

7. A __theory__ is an explanation of a happening or circumstance that is based on observation, experimentation, and reasoning.

8. __Strain__ theory holds that a lack of access and ability to reach goals by legitimate means leads to crime.

9. __Anomie__ is a condition that results from the breakdown or absence of social norms.

10. __Social process__ theory holds that criminal behavior is the predictable result of an individual's interaction with their environment.

11. __Learning__ theory is the hypothesis that delinquents and criminals must be taught both the practical and emotional skills necessary to participate in illegal activity.

12. Labeling can lead to __Self-fulfilling__ prophecy.

13. Practitioners of __life course__ believe that lying, stealing, bullying, and other conduct problems that occur in childhood are the strongest predictors of future criminal behavior.

14. Poor self-control can usually be attributed to poor __parenting__.

15. The __medical__ model of addiction posits that addicts are not criminals.

16. The study of relationships between victims and offenders and victims and the criminal justice system is __victimology__.

17. The idea (Wolfgang's research) that a small group is really responsible for the majority of crime is called the chronic __6%__.

18. The idea that certain people are more likely to be victimized than others is called __repeat victimization__

Short Essays

1. Discuss the difference between a hypothesis and a theory in the context of criminology.

2. Explain why classical criminology is based on choice theory.

3. Contrast positivism with classical criminology.

4. List and describe the three theories of social structure that help explain crime.

5. List and briefly explain the three branches of social process theory.

6. Describe how life course criminology differs from other theories addressed in this chapter.

7. Discuss the connection between offenders and victims of crime.

8. Contrast the medical model of addiction with the criminal model of addiction.

9. Explain the theory of the chronic offender and its importance for the criminal justice system.

Answer Key

True-False:
1. T, see pg. 39, LO1
2. F, see pg. 63, LO8
3. T, see pg. 41, LO3
4. T, see pg. 42, LO3
5. T, see pgs. 43-44, LO3
6. T, see pg. 45, LO3
7. T, see pg. 47, LO3
8. T, see pg. 63, LO8
9. F, see pg. 49, LO4
10. T, see pg. 50, LO4
11. F, see pg. 50, LO4
12. T, see pg. 51, LO5
13. F, see pg. 53, LO5
14. T, see pg. 54, LO5
15. T, see pg. 54, LO5
16. T, see pg. 57, LO6
17. T, see pg. 61, LO7
18. F, see pg. 57, LO7

Multiple Choice:
1. d, see pg. 39, LO1
2. a, see pg. 39, LO1
3. a, see pg. 42, LO3
4. a, see pg. 44, LO3
5. c, see pgs. 46-47, LO3
6. d, see pg. 48, LO4.
7. b, see pg. 63, LO8
8. d, see pg. 51, LO5
9. b, see pg. 53, LO5
10. a, see pg. 54, LO5
11. a, see pg. 41, LO2
12. a, see pg. 41, LO2
13. c, see pg. 58, LO7
14. a, see pg. 54, LO5
15. b, see pg. 58, LO7
16. a, see pg. 41, LO2
17. d, see pgs. 45-46, LO2
18. a, see pgs. 46-47, LO3
19. c, see pg.58, LO6
20. d, see pg.50, LO4
21. b, see pg.65, LO9
22. c, see pgs. 48-49, LO4
23. b, see pg.53, LO4

24. c, see pg.59, LO7
25. a, see pg. 60, LO7

Fill in the Blank:
1. correlation, see pg. 39, LO1
2. free will, see pg. 41, LO1
3. rational choice, see pg. 42, LO1
4. genes, see pg. 44, LO3
5. testosterone, see pg. 45, LO2
6. dopamine, see pg. 45, LO3
7. theory, see pg. 39, LO1
8. strain, see pg. 50, LO4
9. anomie, see pg. 50, LO4
10. social process, see pg. 51, LO5
11. learning, see pg. 51, LO5
12. self-fulfilling, see pg. 53, LO5
13. life course, see pg. 57, LO6
14. parenting, see pg. 57, LO6
15. medical, see pg. 63, LO6.
16. victimology, see pg. 58, LO7
17. chronic 6 percent, see pg. 65, LO9
18. repeat victimization, see pg. 59, LO7

Short Essays:
1. See pgs. 39-40, LO1
2. See pgs. 41-42, LO2
3. See pg. 42, LO3
4. See pgs. 48-51, LO4
5. See pgs. 51-54, LO5
6. See pgs. 57-58, LO6
7. See pgs. 58-60, LO7
8. See pg. 63, LO8
9. See pgs. 65-66, LO9

CHAPTER 3

DEFINING AND MEASURING CRIME

OUTLINE

- Classification of Crimes
- The Uniform Crime Report
- Alternative Measuring Methods
- Crime Trends Today
- Criminal Justice in Action—Legalizing Drugs

Learning Objectives

After reading this chapter, you should be able to:

LO1: Discuss the primary goals of civil law and criminal law and explain how these goals are realized.

LO2: Explain the differences between crimes *mala in se* and *mala prohibita*.

LO3: Identify the publication in which the FBI reports crime data and list the three ways in which the data are reported.

L04: Distinguish between Part I and Part II offenses as defined in the Uniform Crime Report (UCR).

LO5: Describe some of the shortcomings of the UCR as a crime-measuring tool.

LO6: Distinguish between the National Crime Victimization Survey (NCVS) and self-reported surveys.

LO7: Identify the three factors most often used by criminologists to explain increases and declines in the nation's crime rate.

LO8: Explain why issues of race and ethnicity tend to be overstated when it comes to crime trends.

LO9: Discuss the prevailing explanation for the rising number of women incarcerated in the United States.

Chapter Outline

I. Classification of Crimes
    A. Civil Law and Criminal Law
        a. Civil law – the branch of law dealing with the definition and enforcement of all private or public rights, as opposed to criminal matters
        b. Plaintiff – person or institution that initiates a lawsuit in civil court proceedings by filing a complaint
        c. Defendant – in civil court, the person or institution against whom an action is brought. In criminal court, the person or entity that has been formally accused of violating criminal law
        1. Guilt and Responsibility
            a. Liability – in civil court, legal responsibility for one's own or another's actions
        2. The Burden of Proof
            a. Beyond a Reasonable Doubt – the degree of proof required to find the defendant in a criminal trial guilty of committing the crime
    B. Felonies and Misdemeanors
        a. Felony – a serious crime, usually punishable by death or imprisonment for a year or longer
            i. 4 degrees:
                01. Capital offenses, for which maximum penalty is death

38

02. First degree, punishable by maximum of life in prison
03. Second degree, maximum of ten years in prison
04. Third degree, maximum of five years in prison
2. Degrees of crime
3. Types of Manslaughter
    a. Voluntary – homicide which the intent to kill was present in the mind of offender, but malice was lacking
    b. Involuntary – negligent homicide, no intent to kill on part of offender
4. Degrees of Misdemeanor
    a. Misdemeanor – criminal offense that is not a felony usually punishable by a fine and/or jail term of less than one year
5. Infractions
    a. Infraction – a noncriminal offense for which the penalty is a fine rather than incarceration
C. Mala In Se and Mala Prohibita
    a. Mala In Se – acts that are inherently wrong, regardless of whether they are prohibited by law
    b. Mala Prohibita – acts that are made illegal by criminal statute and are not necessarily wrong in and of themselves
2. Making the Distinction
3. The Drug Dilemma
    i. Licit drugs – legal drugs or substances, such as alcohol, caffeine, and nicotine
    ii. Illicit drugs – certain drugs or substances whose use or sale has been declared illegal
    a. Distinguishing between Licit and Illicit Drugs
    b. Society and the Law
II. The Uniform Crime Report (UCR)
    a. Crimes known to the police
    b. Published by the F.B.I.—Crime in the United States
    c. Approximately 17,500 agencies reporting
    d. Contents
        i. As a rate per 100,000 people
        ii. As a percentage change from prior year
        iii. As an aggregate
A. Part I Offenses
1. Part I offenses:
    a. Criminal Homicide
    b. Forcible Rape
    c. Robbery
    d. Aggravated Assault
    e. Burglary—Breaking and Entering
    f. Larceny/Theft
    g. Motor Vehicle Theft

B. Part II Offenses
   1. All other offenses that are not part I
C. The UCR: A Flawed Method?
   1. Discretionary distortions
   2. Clearance distortions
      a. Clearance of an Arrest – occurs when the arrested suspect is charged with a crime and handed over to court for prosecution
D. National Incident-Based Reporting System
   1. started in 1980s (NIBRS)
   2. Four data sets:
      a. Offenses
      b. Victims
      c. Offenders
      d. Arrestees
III. Alternative Measuring Methods
   A. Victim Surveys
      1. National Crime Victimization Survey
         a. Why superior to the UCR:
            i. Measures reported and unreported crime (the dark figure of crime)
            ii. Unaffected by the police bias in UCR
            iii. Does not rely on victim's direct police report
      2. Reliability of the NCVS
         a. Vagueness
         b. Dishonesty on the part of the victim
      3. Further Drawbacks of Victim Surveys
         a. Lack of victim legal knowledge
         b. Some crimes cannot be reported
   B. Self-Reported Surveys
      a. A method of gathering crime data that relies on participants to reveal and detail their own criminal or delinquent behavior
      1. A "Giant" Dark Figure
         a. Possibly catches much more of the actual crime
      2. Reliability of Self-Reported Surveys
         a. Exaggeration by "wannabe" bad people
         b. Hidden crimes by fearful people
IV. Crime Trends in the United States
   A. On the Rise: Crime in the 1960s and 1970s
      a. Usual suspects of crime fluctuation:
         i. Imprisonment
         ii. Youth populations
         iii. The economy
      2. Age and Crime: The Peak Years
      3. Crime and the Economy
   B. Drug Wars: Crime in the 1980s
      1. The Impact of Crack

40

2. The Methamphetamine Scourge
   a. Methamphetamine – synthetic stimulant that creates a strong feeling of euphoria in the user and is highly addictive
3. An Alternative View
C. Looking Good: Crime in the 1990s and 2000s
   1. The Great Crime Decline
      a. Homicide dropped 39%
      b. Robbery dropped 44%
      c. Burglary dropped 41%
      d. Auto theft dropped 37%
   2. Leveling Off
      a. Since 2000
   3. The Immediate Future
D. Crime, Race, and Poverty
   1. Race and Crime
      a. Race and crime are related
         i. Subculture wars
   2. Class and Crime
      a. Income level is more important than skin color when it comes to crime trends
   3. Ethnicity and crime
E. Women and Crime
   a. Crime is an overwhelmingly male activity
   b. Women's crime is growing
      i. Possible explanations:
         01. The life circumstances and behavior of women have changed dramatically in the past 40 years
         02. Criminal justice system's attitude toward women has changed
V. Criminal Justice in Action—Legalizing Drugs

Key Terms

Beyond a reasonable doubt (pg. 76)
Civil law (pg. 75)
Clearance of an arrest (pg. 85)
Dark Figure of Crime (pg. 86)
Defendant (pg. 75)
Felony (pg. 76)
Illicit drugs (pg. 79)
Infraction (pg. 78)
Involuntary manslaughter (pg. 77)
Liability (pg. 75)
Licit drugs (pg. 79)
Mala in se (pg. 78)

Mala prohibita (pg. 78)
Methamphetamine (Meth) (pg. 92)
Misdemeanor (pg. 78)
Part I offenses (pg. 82)
Part II offenses (pg.83)
Plaintiff (pg. 75)
Self-reported surveys (p. 88)
Uniform Crime Report (UCR) (pg. 81)
Victim Surveys (pg. 86)
Voluntary manslaughter (pg. 77)

Special Projects

1. Using popular media, research a criminal homicide case in which an offender was convicted of murder beyond a reasonable doubt. Outline the case and identify the elements of the crime and the evidence used to convict the offender. In your opinion, was the prosecution's proof sufficient for the conviction? Did it equate to proof beyond a reasonable doubt?

2. Talk with a criminal attorney to learn how he or she perceives the adequacy of the criminal law to deal with today's modern crimes (e.g., Internet crimes, harassing text messages, etc...). What does the attorney think should be changed, if anything? Prepare a one-page report on your interview.

3. Select a law enforcement agency (state, local, or county) that reports its crime data to the FBI for the UCR. Briefly summarize the prior year's Part I and Part II crime data for your selected jurisdiction. What is your overall perception of the crime problem in your selected community?

Practice Test

True-False

_____T_1.   The National Incident-Based Reporting System presents a more complete picture of crime than the UCR.

_____F_2.   The *dark figure of crime* refers to the period between 1878-1910 in which corruption plagued police agencies and the crime rate exploded.

_____F_3.   Murder, rape, and theft are examples of *mala prohibita* crimes.

_T_ 4. The UCR presents data on the number of people who are arrested each year.

_T_ 5. Part I offenses are the more serious offenses tracked in the UCR.

_T_ 6. Part II offenses may include both felonies and misdemeanors.

_T_ 7. In low-income neighborhoods, the rate of violent crime is more highly associated with family disorganization than with race.

_T_ 8. The strongest statistical determinant of criminal behavior appears to be age.

_T_ 9. Research reveals that women are involved in a narrow band of wrongdoing mostly involving drug, property, and alcohol offenses.

_F_ 10. Civil lawsuits are normally initiated by public prosecutors.

Multiple Choice

1. Which of the following is an element of first degree murder?
   a. Premeditation
   b. Intuition
   c. Provocation
   d. Passion

2. The Uniform Crime Report (UCR) is considered flawed for all of the following reasons EXCEPT
   a. lack of full citizen reporting.
   b. police underreporting.
   c. differential interpretations.
   d. lack of political support.

3. When the intent to kill is present, but malice aforethought is lacking, the crime is
   a. first degree murder.
   b. second degree murder.
   c. voluntary manslaughter.
   d. involuntary manslaughter.

4. The Uniform Crime Report (UCR) includes
   a. the number of people arrested by police each year.
   b. the number of people victimized by crime each year.
   c. the number of people convicted of crimes each year.
   d. the number of people who break the law each year.

43

5. Which format is NOT utilized by the Uniform Crime Report (UCR) to report data?
    a. Rates
    b. Percentage change over time
    c. Aggregate totals
    d. Summation totals

6. NIBRS is an acronym that stands for
    a. National Individual Offense Register System.
    b. National Individualized-Record System.
    c. National Incident Recording System.
    d. National Incident-Based Reporting System.

7. The NCVS
    a. measures arrest rates.
    b. measures victimization rates.
    c. measures offending rates.
    d. measures conviction rates.

8. Today illicit and licit drugs are regulated under the
    a. Controlled Chemical Act.
    b. Controlled Substance Act.
    c. Narcotic and Dependant drug Act.
    d. Drug Addict Schedule Act.

9. The burden of proof in civil court is
    a. beyond a reasonable doubt.
    b. clear and convincing evidence.
    c. preponderance of the evidence.
    d. probable cause.

10. When an act of violence is planned and decided upon after a process of decision making, it is
    a. premeditated.
    b. deliberate.
    c. malice aforethought.
    d. negligence.

11. Which of the following is considered a *mala prohibita* offense?
    a. Murder
    b. Prostitution
    c. Theft
    d. Rape

44

12. Misdemeanors are generally punishable by a fine and/or
    a. the assignment of punitive damages.
    b. one or more years in prison.
    c. confinement to jail for up to one year.
    d. punishable by forfeiture of property.

13. Which one is NOT a Part II UCR offense?
    a. Drunk Driving
    b. Vagrancy
    c. Gambling
    d. Arson

14. Which one is NOT a Part I UCR offense?
    a. Aggravated assault
    b. Larceny-theft
    c. Embezzlement
    d. Arson

15. The dark figure of crime refers to
    a. the actual amount of crime taking place.
    b. the actual number of crimes reported to police.
    c. the fact that all offenses in a crime spree are reported.
    d. only felony crimes against persons.

16. According to the text, what drug is considered to be the most serious drug problem in the United States?
    a. Crack cocaine
    b. Heroin
    c. Marijuana
    d. Methamphetamine

17. Which of the following is NOT associated with juvenile delinquency?
    a. Testosterone level
    b. Peer pressure
    c. Education
    d. Age

18. In a criminal court, the person or entity who has been formally accused of violating a criminal law is the
    a. prosecutor.
    b. plaintiff.
    c. defendant.
    d. appellant.

19. Civil law involves
     a. offenses against the state.
     b. offenses against society.
     c. guilt or innocence.
     d. liability. *(circled)*

20. Which is the fastest growing segment of the U.S. prison population?
     a. Women
     b. African-Americans
     c. Hispanic-Americans *(circled)*
     d. Juveniles

Fill in the Blank

1. The branch of law dealing with disputes between private entities is
   _____civil_____ law.

2. Offenses against society as a whole are the subject of the
   _____criminal_____ law.

3. Generally, crimes punishable the death penalty or imprisonment in excess of
   one year are classified as _____felonies_____.

4. The killing of a person with a negligent act and no intent is _____manslaughter_____.

5. The term _____mala prohibita_____ refers to acts that are considered crimes only
   because they have been codified as such through statute.

6. The _____UCR_____ is an annual report compiled by the FBI
   that portrays overall criminal activity in the United States.

7. Part I and Part II offenses are indicated in the _____UCR_____.

8. When crime is reported in terms of "for every 100,000 inhabitants of the United
   States", this statistic is known as the _____crime rate_____.

9. _____Self_____ reports rely on participants to reveal and detail their
   own criminal or delinquent behavior.

10. In _____victim surveys_____, criminologists or other researchers ask the
    victims of crime directly about their experiences, using techniques such as
    interviews or electronic mail and phone surveys.

Short Essays

1. Compare and contrast civil law and criminal law.

2. Explain the differences between crimes *mala in se* and *mala prohibita*.

3. Identify the publication in which the FBI reports crime data and list the three ways in which the data are reported.

47

4. Distinguish between Part I and Part II offenses as defined in the Uniform Crime Report (UCR).

5. Describe some of the shortcomings of the UCR as a crime-measuring tool.

6. Distinguish between the National Crime Victimization Survey (NCVS) and self-reported surveys.

7. Identify the three factors most often used by criminologists to explain increases and declines in the nation's crime rate.

8. Explain why issues of race and ethnicity tend to be overstated when it comes to crime trends.

9. Discuss the prevailing explanation for the rising number of women incarcerated in the United States.

49

Answer Key

True-False:
1. T, see pgs. 85-86, LO5
2. F, see pg. 86, LO5
3. F, see pg. 78, LO2
4. T, see pg. 82, LO3
5. T, see pg. 82, LO4
6. T, see pg. 83, LO4
7. T, see pg. 95, LO8
8. T, see pg. 91, LO7
9. T, see pg. 97, LO9
10. F, see pg. 75, LO1

Multiple Choice:
1. a, see pg. 77, LO2
2. d, see pgs. 84-85, LO5
3. c, see pg. 77, LO2
4. a, see pg. 82, LO3
5. d, see pg. 82, LO3
6. d, see pg. 85, LO5
7. b, see pg. 86, LO6
8. b, see pg. 80, LO2
9. c, see pg. 76, LO1
10. b, see pg. 77, LO1
11. b, see pg. 78, LO2
12. c, see pg. 78, LO2
13. d, see pg. 84, LO4
14. c, see pg. 83, LO4
15. a, see pg. 88, LO5
16. d, see pg. 92, LO7.
17. c, see pg. 91, LO7
18. c, see pg. 75, LO1
19. d, see pg. 75, LO1
20. c, see pg. 97, LO8.

Fill in the Blank:
1. civil, see pg. 75, LO1
2. criminal, see pg. 75, LO1
3. felonies, see pg. 76, LO1
4. manslaughter, see pg. 77, LO1
5. *mala prohibita*, see pg. 78, LO2.
6. UCR, see pg. 81, LO3
7. UCR, see pgs. 81-82, LO4
8. crime rate, see pg. 82, LO3
9. self, see pg. 88, LO6
10. victim surveys, see pg. 86, LO6

Short Essays:
1. See pgs. 75-76, LO1
2. See pgs. 78-79, LO2
3. See pg. 81, LO3
4. See pgs. 82-84, LO4
5. See pgs. 83-85, LO5
6. See pgs. 86-89, LO6
7. See pgs. 92-93, LO7
8. See pgs. 95-96, LO8
9. See pgs. 97-98, LO9

CHAPTER 4

INSIDE CRIMINAL LAW

OUTLINE

- The Development of American Criminal Law
- Written Sources of American Criminal Law
- The Purposes of a Criminal Law
- The Elements of a Crime
- Defenses under Criminal Law
- Procedural Safeguards
- Criminal Justice in Action—"Stand Your Ground" or "Shoot First"?

Learning Objectives

After reading this chapter, you should be able to:

LO1: Explain precedent and the importance of the doctrine of *stare decisis.*
LO2: List the four written sources of United States criminal law.
LO3: Explain the two basic functions of criminal law.
LO4: Delineate the elements required to establish *mens rea* (a guilty mental state).
LO5: Explain how the doctrine of strict liability applies to criminal law.
LO6: List and briefly define the most important excuse defenses for crimes.
LO7: Describe the four most important justification criminal defenses.
LO8: Distinguish between substantive and procedural criminal law.
LO9: Explain the importance of the due process clause in the criminal justice system.

Chapter Outline

I. The Development of American Criminal Law
   A. The conception of law
      1. Understanding the term "law."
      2. Sources of modern law.
   B. English Common Law
      a. Common law – the body of law developed from custom or judicial decisions in English and U.S. Courts and not attributable to a legislature
      b. Precedent – a court decision that furnishes an example of authority for deciding subsequent cases involving similar facts
     1. *Stare Decisis*
      a. A common law doctrine under which judges are obligated to follow the precedents established under prior decisions
II. Written Sources of American Criminal Law
      a. Include:
         i. U.S. and state constitutions
         ii. Statutes:
            01. Congress
            02. State legislatures
            03. Local ordinances
         iii. Regulations
            01. Regulatory agencies
         iv. Case Law
            01. Court decisions
   A. Constitutional Law
      1. Supreme law of the land

B. Statutory Law
    a. Must comply with the Constitution
    b. Common Law and the State Statutes
   1. The Influence of Common Law
   2. Model Penal Code
    a. A statutory text created by the American Law Institute that sets forth general principles of criminal responsibility and defines specific offenses
   3. Ballot Initiatives
    a. Voters can write or rewrite criminal statutes
C. Administrative Law
   1. State and federal agencies are empowered to create rules in order to carry out their duties and responsibilities
D. Case Law
   1. From the Common Law tradition

III. The Purposes of Criminal Law
  A. Protect and Punish: The Legal Function of the Law
   1. Prevent harms to citizens
   2. Prevent harms to society's interests
  B. Maintain and Teach: The Social Function of the Law
   1. Expressing Public Morality
   2. Teaching Societal Boundaries

IV. The Elements of a Crime
    a. Corpus Delicti
     i. The body of circumstances that must exist for a criminal act to have occurred
     ii. Consists of the basic elements of any crime:
      01. Guilty act
      02. Guilty intent
      03. Concurrence
      04. Link between the act and the legal definition of the crime
      05. Any attendant circumstances
      06. The harm done, or result of the criminal act
  A. Criminal Act: *Actus Reus*
    a. A guilty (prohibited) act
    b. Commission
   1. A Legal Duty
    a. Omission
   2. A Plan or Attempt
    a. Attempt – act of taking substantial steps toward committing a crime while having the ability and the intent to commit the crime, even if the crime never takes place
  B. Mental State: *Mens Rea*
    a. *Mens rea* – mental state, or intent
   1. The Categories of *Mens Rea*
    a. Purpose

      b. Knowledge
      c. Recklessness
      d. Negligence
  2. Criminal Liability
  3. Strict Liability
      i. Certain crimes, such as traffic violations, in which the defendant is guilty regardless of her or his state of mind at the time of the act
      a. Protecting the Public
      b. Protecting minors
        i. Statutory rape – an adult engages in a sexual relationship with a minor
  4. Accomplice Liability
      a. Must have dual intent:
        i. To aid the person who committed the crime
        ii. Such aid would lead to the commission of the crime
      b. Felony-murder – an unlawful homicide that occurs during the attempted commission of a felony
C. Concurrence
D. Causation
E. Attendant Circumstances
      a. The facts surrounding a criminal event
  1. Requirements of Proof and Intent
  2. Hate crime laws
      i. A statute that provides for greater sanctions against those who commit crimes motivated by bias against an individual or group based on race, ethnicity, religion, gender, sexual orientation, disability, or age
      a. Supreme Court Support
      b. Questioning Hate Laws
F. Harm
      a. Inchoate offenses – conduct deemed criminal without actual harm being done, provided that the harm would have occurred is one the law tries to prevent
V. Defenses under Criminal Law
      a. Defenses generally rely on one of two arguments:
        i. Defendant is not responsible for the crime
        ii. Defendant was justified in committing the crime
A. Criminal Responsibility and the Law
  1. Defendant not responsible
      a. Infancy
        i. Condition that, under early American law, excused young wrongdoers of criminal behavior because presumably they could not understand the consequences of their actions
      b. Insanity

01. A defense for criminal liability that asserts a lack of criminal responsibility
  i. Measuring Insanity
    01. Person is excused from crime if as a result of mental disease or defect:
      - Does not perceive the physical nature or consequences of conduct
      - Does not know conduct is wrong or criminal
      - Is not sufficiently able to control conduct to be accountable for it
    02. Tests of insanity:
      - M'Naughten Rule
      - Irresistible Impulse Test
      - Substantial Capacity Test
  ii. Determining Competency
    01. Competency hearing – a court proceeding to determine whether the defendant is mentally well enough to understand the charges filed against him and cooperate with a lawyer in presenting a defense
  iii. Guilty but mentally ill
c. Intoxication
  i. Two types:
    01. Voluntary
    02. Involuntary
d. Mistake
  i. Mistake of law
    01. Law was not published or reasonably known to the public
    02. Person relied on an official statement of the law that was erroneous
  ii. Mistake of fact
B. Justification Criminal Defenses and the Law
  1. Duress
    a. Unlawful pressure brought to bear on a person, causing the person to perform an act that he or she would not otherwise perform
    b. To qualify duress must be:
      i. Threat must be of serious bodily harm or death
      ii. Harm threatened must be greater than the harm caused by the crime
      iii. Threat must be immediate and inescapable
      iv. Defendant must have become involved in the situation through no fault of his own
  2. Justifiable Use of Force – Self-Defense
    i. Reasonably necessary to protect one's self or property
    ii. Duty to retreat
      01. Applies only in public spaces and

55

    02. Does not apply when the force used in self-defense was nondeadly

  3. Necessity

   a. Defendant asserts that circumstances required to commit an illegal act

  4. Entrapment

   i. Defendant claims he was induced by a public official to commit a crime that he would otherwise not have committed

   a. The Whiskey Case

   b. The Pornography Case

VI. Procedural Safeguards

  a. Substantive criminal law – law that defines the rights and duties of individuals with respect to each other

  b. Procedural criminal law – rules that define the manner in which the rights and duties of individuals may be enforced

 A. The Bill of Rights

  a. First ten Amendments

  1. Amending the Constitution

   a. The Fourth Amendment—unreasonable search and seizure

    i. Warrants require probable cause

   b. The Fifth Amendment—no loss of life, liberty, or property without due process

    i. No double jeopardy

    ii. No self-incrimination

   c. The Sixth Amendment—speedy trial

    i. Trial by jury

    ii. Public trial

    iii. Confront witnesses

    iv. Right to an attorney

   d. Eighth Amendment—no excessive bails or fines

    i. No cruel and unusual punishments

  2. Expanding the Constitution

 B. Due Process

  a. Due Process Clause – the provisions of the Fifth and Fourteenth Amendments to the Constitution that guarantee that no person shall be deprived of life, liberty, or property with due process of law

  1. Procedural Due Process

   a. A provision in the Constitution that states that the law must be carried out in a fair and orderly manner

  2. Substantive Due Process

   a. The constitutional requirement that laws used in accusing and convicting persons of crimes must be fair

  3. The Supreme Court's Role in Due Process

  4. Challenges to Due Process

   a. Due Process and National Security

VII. Criminal Justice in Action – "Stand Your Ground" or "Shoot First"

Key Terms

Actus reus (pg. 119)
Administrative law (pg. 114)
Attempt (pg. 120)
Attendant circumstances (pg. 123)
Bill of Rights (pg. 134)
Case law (pg. 114)
Common law (pg. 109)
Competency hearing (pg. 128)
Constitutional law (pg. 111)
Corpus Delicti (pg. 118)
Due process clause (pg. 135)
Duress (pg. 130)
Duty to retreat (pg. 131)
Entrapment (pg. 132)
Felony-murder (pg. 122)
Hate Crime law (pg. 124)
Inchoate offenses (pg. 125)
Infancy (pg. 126)
Insanity (pg. 126)
Intoxication (pg. 128)
Irresistible-impulse test (pg. 127)
Mens Rea (pg. 120)
M'Naghten Rule (pg. 127)
Model Penal Code (pg. 113)
Necessity (pg. 132)
Negligence (pg. 120)
Precedent (pg. 110)
Procedural criminal law (pg. 134)
Procedural due process (pg. 135)
Recklessness (pg. 120)
Self-defense (pg. 131)
Stare decisis (pg. 110)
Statutory law (pg. 112)
Statutory rape (pg. 122)
Strict liability (pg. 121)
Substantial-capacity test (pg. 127)
Substantive criminal law (pg. 134)
Substantive due process (pg. 137)

Special Projects

1. Watch an episode of Law and Order© and take notes during the show. Using the list of key terms above, how many terms or concepts did you identify during the show? For example:
- Procedural law - did police search a suspect or interview a suspect?
- Case law - did attorneys make reference to case law during the show?

After you have compared the key terms / concepts list to the episode, prepare a brief report about what you were able to identify.

2. Using the Internet, research a criminal case in which a defendant was charged with a hate crime. Prepare a case outline identifying the facts of the case and its outcome. Cite the specific charge and identify the jurisdiction.

3. If you were a legislator, what law would you like to propose or add to the existing laws? Draft your law and affix the penalty or sanction for a violation of your law. What motivated you to draft your specific law?

Practice Test

True-False

___T___ 1. The law consists of enforceable rules governing relationships among individuals and between individuals and their society.

___F___ 2. English common law derived exclusively from English customs.

___T___ 3. The U.S. Constitution is considered to be the supreme law of the land.

___F___ 4. Statutory law is also known as judge-made law.

___T___ 5. The primary functions of the law are to protect citizens from harm and to maintain social order.

___T___ 6. The proof that a specific crime has actually been committed by someone is known as the *corpus delicti*.

___F___ 7. Attendant circumstances must be proved beyond a reasonable doubt.

___T___ 8. Under the rules of accomplice liability; a person can be charged with and convicted of a crime that he or she didn't actually commit.

58

_F_ 9. Courts accept any form of intoxication as a viable defense.

_T_ 10. Mistake as an excuse defense can be either (1) mistake of fact or (2) mistake of law.

_T_ 11. Duress is unlawful pressure brought to bear upon a person that causes the person to perform an act that they would not have performed otherwise.

_T_ 12. Substantive criminal law essentially defines the acts that the government will punish.

_F_ 13. The first ten amendments to the U. S. Constitution are known as the *Preamble*.

_F_ 14. Entrapment is an excuse defense.

_F_ 15. The Fourteenth Amendment provides protection from cruel and unusual punishment.

_F_ 16. Recklessness is the failure to exercise the standard of care that other persons would exercise in a similar situation.

Multiple Choice

1. Common law
   a. is a collected work of law comprised of state constitutions---and as such came to be the law of the land.
   b. infused religious law and mores which ultimately became legislated law.
   c. is law derived from customs and judicial decisions not attributable to a legislature.
   d. is the law established by the King for his commoners.

2. The doctrine of *stare decisis*
   a. is the precursor to our U.S. Constitution.
   b. was established by the church as a means of dealing with moral dilemmas.
   c. prohibits prosecution of a person under the age of seven.
   d. is the practice of deciding new cases with reference to precedent.

3. The written sources of substantive U.S. law includes all of the following EXCEPT
    a. common law.
    b. regulations of federal agencies.
    c. case law.
    d. statutory law

4. Administrative law is created by
    a. the Congress as part of its regulatory responsibility.
    b. the Senate Judicial Committee.
    c. the judicial branch of government.
    d. the government's administrative agencies.

5. The social function of the law is to
    a. protect individuals from criminal harm.
    b. punish those who break the law.
    c. define social boundaries.
    d. protect society's interest against unsafe consumer products and pollution.

6. *Corpus delicti* is defined as
    a. the circumstances necessary for a crime to have occurred.
    b. a human corpse that is the subject of a homicide investigation.
    c. the intent in a criminal act.
    d. the process by which case law becomes actual precedent.

7. Which category of *mens rea* involves gross deviation from the standard of care a reasonable person would provide?
    a. Negligence
    b. Willfulness
    c. Recklessness
    d. Knowledge

8. Which of the following is a common law test of insanity that relies on a defendant's inability to distinguish right from wrong?
    a. Substantial Capacity test
    b. M'Naghten rule
    c. Dorman rule
    d. Irresistible impulse test

9. Which of the following is a justification defense?
    a. Insanity
    b. Self-defense
    c. Infancy
    d. Intoxication

10. Which Amendment extends due process protections to the states?
   a. Fourth Amendment
   b. Sixth Amendment
   c. Eighth Amendment
   d. Fourteenth Amendment

11. The Constitutional requirement that the law be carried out in a fair and orderly manner is known as
   a. procedural due process.
   b. substantive due process.
   c. the Bill of Rights.
   d. administrative law.

12. Corpus delicti requires concurrence, which means
   a. the guilty act must be the cause of the harm suffered.
   b. the guilty act and the harm must occur at the same time.
   c. the guilty act and the guilty intent must come together.
   d. the guilty act must not only be attempted, but completed.

13. The FDA, OSHA, and the EPA are examples of
   a. law enforcement agencies.
   b. internal review agencies.
   c. regulatory agencies.
   d. civil law legislative agencies

14. The Model Penal Code is a statutory text created by the American law Institute that sets forth
   a. case law.
   b. general principles of criminal responsibility.
   c. administrative law.
   d. constitutional law.

15. The elements of a crime include all of the following EXCEPT
   a. concurrence.
   b. *actus reus*.
   c. *mens rea*.
   d. *stare decisis*.

16. Attendant circumstances are
   a. the facts or accompanying circumstances of a case.
   b. the factors that serve to mitigate harm.
   c. those that require criminal intent.
   d. required in all criminal cases.

61

17. Which one is NOT a requirement as part of a duress defense?
    a. The threat must be of serious bodily harm or death
    b. The harm threatened must be greater than the harm caused by the crime
    c. The threat must be immediate and inescapable
    d. The defendant must have entered into the situation willfully

18. The Sixth Amendment provides
    a. for a speedy trial.
    b. protection against unreasonable search and seizure.
    c. protection from excessive fines or punishments.
    d. due process protections to the states.

19. The Eighth Amendment provides
    a. for a speedy trial.
    b. protection against unreasonable search and seizure.
    c. protection from excessive fines or punishments.
    d. due process protections to the states.

20. Due process is ultimately determined by the
    a. trial judge.
    b. trial lawyer.
    c. American Bar Association.
    d. U.S. Supreme Court.

21. The guidelines for determining entrapment were established in
    a. *Duane C. v. United States.*
    b. *Gerber v. United States.*
    c. *Whiskey v. United States.*
    d. *Sorrells v. United States.*

22. Stare decisis is a common law doctrine
    a. requiring judges to follow precedent.
    b. requiring adherence to lex talionis.
    c. taken directly from the Code of Hammurabi.
    d. taken directly from the Mosaic Code.

23. The primary function of the law is to protect, punish and
    a. rehabilitate.
    b. express public morality.
    c. reflect the values and norms of society.
    d. regulate human behavior.

62

24. *Actus reus* is the
    a. guilty act.
    b. guilty mind.
    c. elements of a crime.
    d. presence of criminal culpability.

25. Which crime is an example of a strict liability crime?
    a. Murder
    b. Statutory rape
    c. Gambling
    d. Arson

Fill in the Blank

1. A guilty mental state is known as ___mens rea___.

2. A court decision that furnishes an example of authority for determining future cases is called ___precedent___.

3. Statutes enacted by legislative bodies at any level of government are called ___statutory___ law.

4. Though not a law itself, the ___Model Penal Code___ defines the general principles of criminal responsibility and codifies specific offenses.

5. The rule of law announced in court decisions is ___case___ law.

6. The body of circumstances that must exist for a criminal act to have occurred is ___corpus delicti___.

7. The Latin term used to refer to "the commission of a prohibited act" is ___actus reus___.

8. In a ___strict liability___ crime, the defendant is guilty regardless of her or his state of mind at the time of the act.

9. ___Insanity___ is a defense for criminal liability that asserts a lack of criminal responsibility.

10. Unlawful pressure which causes a person to commit a criminal act, one that they would not otherwise perform, is ___duress___.

11. The law that defines the rights and duties of individuals in relation to each other is ___substantive___ criminal law.

12. Rules that define the manner in which the rights and duties of individuals may be enforced are ___procedural___ criminal law.

13. A statute that provides for greater sanctions against those who commit crimes motivated by bias against an individual or a group based on race, ethnicity, religion, gender, sexual orientation, disability, or age is called ___hate crime___ law.

14. Conduct deemed criminal without actual harm being done, provided that the harm that would have occurred is one the law tries to prevent is a(n) ___inchoate___ offense.

15. The Fourteenth Amendment extends due process rights to the ___states___ .

16. Duress, self-defense, and necessity are examples of ___justification___ defenses.

Short Essays

1. Explain precedent and the doctrine of *stare decisis*.

2. List the four written sources of United States criminal law.

3. Explain the two basic functions of criminal law.

4. Delineate the elements required to establish *mens rea* (a guilty mental state).

5. Explain how the doctrine of strict liability applies to criminal law.

6. List and briefly define the most important excuse defenses for crimes.

7. Describe the four most important justification criminal defenses.

8. Distinguish between substantive and procedural criminal law.

66

9. Explain the importance of the due process clause in the criminal justice system.

Answer Key

True-False:
1. T, see pg. 109, LO1
2. F, see pg. 109, LO1
3. T, see pg. 112, LO2
4. F, see pg. 112, LO2
5. T, see pg. 115, LO3
6. T, see pg. 118, LO4
7. F, see pg. 123, LO5
8. T, see pg. 122, LO5
9. F, see pg. 128, LO6
10. T, see pgs. 129-130, LO6
11. T, see pg. 130, LO7
12. T, see pg. 134, LO8
13. F, see pg. 134, LO9
14. F, see pg. 132, LO7
15. F, see pg. 135, LO9
16. F, see pg. 120, LO4

Multiple Choice:
1. c, see pg. 109, LO1
2. d, see pg. 110, LO1
3. a, see pg. 111, LO2
4. d, see pg. 114, LO2
5. c, see pg. 116, LO3
6. a, see pg. 118, LO3
7. a, see pg. 120, LO4
8. b, see pg. 127, LO6
9. b, see pg. 133, LO7
10. d, see pg. 137, LO9
11. a, see pg. 135, LO8
12. c, see pg. 123, LO4
13. c, see pg. 114, LO2
14. b, see pg. 113, LO2
15. d, see pg. 118, LO4
16. a, see pg. 123, LO4
17. b, see pg. 132, LO7
18. a, see pg. 135, LO8
19. c, see pg. 135, LO8
20. d, see pg. 136, LO9
21. d, see pg. 132, LO7
22. a, see pg. 110, LO1
23. c, see pg. 116, LO3
24. a, see pg. 119, LO4
25. b, see pg. 122, LO5

Fill in the Blank:
1. *mens rea*, see pg. 120, LO4
2. precedent, see pg. 110, LO1
3. statutory, see pg. 112, LO2
4. Model Penal Code,
    see pg. 113, LO2
5. case, see pg. 114, LO2
6. corpus delicti, see pg. 118, LO4
7. *actus reus*, see pg. 119, LO4
8. strict liability, see pg. 121, LO5
9. Insanity, see pg. 126, LO6
10. duress, see pg 130, LO7
11. substantive, see pg. 134, LO8.
12. procedural, see pg. 134, LO8
13. hate crime, see pg. 124, LO5
14. inchoate, see pg. 125, LO5
15. states, see pg. 134, LO9
16. justification, see pg. 133, LO7

Short Essays:
1. See pg. 110, LO1
2. See pg. 111, LO2
3. See pgs. 115-116, LO3
4. See pg. 118, LO4
5. See pgs. 121-122, LO5
6. See pgs. 125-129, LO6
7. See pgs. 130-133, LO7
8. See pgs. 134-135, LO8
9. See pgs. 135-138, LO9

CHAPTER 5

LAW ENFORCEMENT TODAY

OUTLINE

- A History of the American Police
- The Responsibilities of the Police
- Law Enforcement Agencies
- Private Security
- The Role of Discretion in Policing
- Criminal Justice in Action—Policing Illegal Immigrants

Learning Objectives

After reading this chapter, you should be able to:

LO1: Describe the first systems of law enforcement in colonial America.
LO2: Tell how the patronage system affected policing.
LO3: Indicate the results of the Wickersham Commission.
LO4: List the four basic responsibilities of the police.
LO5: List five main types of law enforcement agencies.
LO6: Indicate some of the most important law enforcement agencies under the control of the Department of Homeland Security.
LO7: Identify the duties of the FBI.
LO8: Analyze the importance of private security today.
LO9: Indicate why patrol officers are allowed discretionary powers.
LO10: Explain how some jurisdictions have reacted to perceived leniency to perpetrators of domestic violence.

Chapter Outline

I.   A History of the American Police
   A. English Roots
     1. Shire-Reeve
     2. Constable
     3. Justice of the Peace
       a. Parish Constable System
     4. London Experiments
       a. "Reading the riot act"
       b. Sir Robert Peel
         i. Metropolitan Police Act of 1829
         ii. "Bobbies"
   B. The Early American Police Experience
     1. The First Police Department
       a. Boston
         i. First formal night watch
       b. Walker's commentary on the quality of American police service
     2. The spoils system
       a. Patronage system – a form of corruption in which the political party in power hires and promotes police officers, receiving job-related "favors" in return
   C. The Modernization of American Police
     1. Professionalism
       a. Professional model – style of policing advocated by August Vollmer and O.W. Wilson that emphasizes centralized police organizations, increased use of technology, and a limitation of police discretion through regulations and guidelines

2. Administrative Reforms
3. Technology
4. Turmoil in the 1960s
    a. National Advisory Commission on Civil Disorders
D. Returning to the Community
    a. Omnibus Crime Control and Safe Streets Act of 1968
    b. Proactive strategies for policing
E. The Challenges of Anti-Terrorism

II. The Responsibilities of the Police
    a. Four basic responsibilities:
        i. Enforce laws
        ii. Provide services
        iii. Prevent crime
        iv. Preserve peace
A. Enforcing Laws
1. Crime Fighters
2. "crook catchers"
B. Providing Services
1. Law Enforcement Code of Ethics
C. Preventing Crime
D. Preserving the Peace
1. Wilson and Kelling—*Broken Windows Theory*

III. Law Enforcement Agencies
A. Municipal Enforcement Agencies
1. Cities and towns
B. Sheriffs and County Law Enforcement
    a. Sheriff – the primary law enforcement officer in a county, usually elected to the post by a popular vote
1. Size and Responsibility of Sheriff's Departments
    a. Investigate crimes in their jurisdiction
    b. Investigating drug crimes
    c. Maintaining the county jail
    d. Carrying out civil and criminal processes
    e. Keeping order in the county courthouse
    f. Collecting taxes
    g. Enforcing orders of the court
2. The County Coroner
    a. The medical examiner of a county, usually elected by popular vote
C. State Police and Highway Patrols
    a. Created for four reasons:
        i. Assist local police agencies
        ii. Investigate criminal activities that cross jurisdictional boundaries
        iii. Provide law enforcement in rural and other areas not covered by local or county agencies
        iv. Break strikes and control labor movements
2. The Difference Between the State Police and Highway Patrols

3. Limited-Purpose Law Enforcement Agencies
D. Federal Law Enforcement Agencies
1. The Department of Homeland Security
   a. U.S. Customs and Border Protection (CBP)
   b. Immigrations and Customs Enforcement (ICE)
   c. U.S. Secret Service
2. Department of Justice
   a. Federal Bureau of Investigation
      i. Responsible for investigating violations of federal law
   b. Drug Enforcement Administration
   c. Bureau of Alcohol, Tobacco, Firearms and Explosives
   d. U.S. Marshals Service
3. Department of the Treasury
   a. Internal Revenue Service
IV. The Military and Law Enforcement
1. The Posse Comitatus Act (PCA)
A. Militarism in Police Culture
1. Special Weapons and Tactics Team – specialized squad of police officers who have been trained to handle violent and dangerous situations using advanced weaponry and technology
B. The National Guard
1. Military reserve units of the U.S. Army and U.S. Air Force controlled by each state
V. Private Security
   a. Practice of private corporations or individuals offering services traditionally performed by police officers
A. Privatizing Law Enforcement
1. Citizens' Arrests
2. The Deterrence Factor
B. Private Security Trends
1. Lack of Standards
2. Continued Growth of Private Security
   a. Four factors driving growth:
      i. An increase in fear on the part of public triggered by media coverage
      ii. Crime in the workplace
      iii. Budget cuts in states and municipalities
      iv. Rising awareness of private security products
VI. The Role of Discretion in Policing
A. Justification for police discretion
B. Making the decision
1. Discretion and Domestic Violence
   a. The problem: Failure to arrest
   b. The response: Mandatory arrest policies

72

       i.   Requires a police officer to detain a person for committing a certain type of crime as long as probable cause that the crime exists

    2. Discretion and High Speed Pursuits

VII.   Criminal Justice in Action—Policing Illegal Immigrants

Key Terms

Coroner (pg. 161)
Federal Bureau of Investigation (FBI) (pg. 165)
Mandatory arrest policy (pg. 175)
National Guard (pg. 170)
Patronage system (pg. 151)
Private security (pg. 170)
Professional model (pg. 152)
Sheriff (pg. 160)
Special Weapons and Tactics (SWAT) Team (pg. 170)

Special Projects

1. Research your local county government and identify whether they utilize a coroner or a medical examiner as the government office for ascertaining the cause of death. Research the history of the office and identify the (1) name of the medical official, (2) the minimum education required for the position, (3) the average annual caseload, (4) some of the services the office provides/performs and, (5) the number of employees that work for the office. Did you learn anything surprising?

2. Use the Internet to do some job hunting; locate at least three unique positions that the FBI is currently seeking candidates for. Describe each position with some detail (at least one paragraph per position) and include basic information such as (1) the title of the position, (2) minimum education requirements, and (3) the location of the vacancy. Does the FBI seem to employ a diverse range of disciplines? Be prepared to present your report to your class.

3. Research your state law enforcement agency (if your state does not have one pick an alternate). Report on the agency's history, agency's size, roles and responsibilities, and their internal rank structure. Do you feel that state police agencies are an important part of the law enforcement community? Are any duties exclusive to the state police agency?

Practice Test

True-False

_T_ 1. The third era in American policing is officially known as the community era.

_T_ 2. The shire-reeve was the precursor to the American sheriff.

_T_ 3. The Wickersham Commission is directly related to the police reform movement.

_F_ 4. The first U.S. police department was established in New York in 1801.

_T_ 5. At times, police officers encounter a task that requires the "multilayering" of law enforcement. For example, a wide network of local, state, and federal agencies working cooperatively.

_T_ 6. The Department of Homeland Security is responsible to coordinate and protect the U.S. against international and domestic terrorism.

_F_ 7. The FBI is the lead investigative agency under the Department of Homeland Security.

_T_ 8. The Secret Service has a uniformed division and a plainclothes division.

_T_ 9. The FBI has primary jurisdiction over two hundred federal crimes including extortion, bank robbery, and interstate gambling.

_T_ 10. The ATF is primarily concerned with illegal sale, possession, and use of firearms and control of untaxed liquor and tobacco products.

_F_ 11. The Department of Justice (DOJ) is the oldest federal law enforcement agency.

_T_ 12. In the eyes of the law, a security guard is the same as any other private person when it comes to police powers such as arrest and interrogation.

_F_ 13. Public police agencies and private policing companies have very similar functions.

_F_ 14. Police administrators, such as a chief, have the greatest amount of discretion within a police agency.

_F_ 15. The National Guard is the only agency associated with the U.S. Military allowed to perform law enforcement duties on U.S. soil.

_T_ 16. Historically, the law enforcement response to domestic violence was to treat it as a "family matter."

Multiple Choice

1. Which of the following was not a part of the Metropolitan Police Act?
   a. Probation period for officers
   b. Training in deadly force policy
   c. Rules for clothing and conduct
   d. Wages commensurate with a time-in-grade (or rank) system

2. The patronage system
   a. was popular with police reformers because it brought ethics and morality to police work.
   b. emphasized professionalism in law enforcement.
   c. emphasized education for law enforcement officers.
   d. was also known as the "spoils system."

3. The police professionalism model is credited to August Vollmer and
   a. George Wickersham.
   b. O.W. Wilson.
   c. Herbert Hoover.
   d. Sir Robert Peel.

4. The three eras of policing include all of the following EXCEPT
   a. the reform era.
   b. the community era.
   c. the political era.
   d. the military era.

5. Sheriffs typically
   a. maintain county jails.
   b. maintain public order within municipalities.
   c. police public highways.
   d. work for the coroner.

6. What is the difference between a state police agency and highway patrol agency?

    a. State police officers have more limited authority as to where and what they can enforce

    b. State police agencies work directly for the state whereas highway patrol agencies work for the local government

    c. Highway patrol officers have more limited authority as to where and what they can enforce

    d. Name is the only difference otherwise they perform the same work

7. Which one would be described as a limited purpose law enforcement organization?

    a. Fish and game enforcement

    b. Coroner's office

    c. Highway patrol

    d. Private security companies

8. Which agency is part of the Department of Homeland Security?

    a. U.S. Secret Service

    b. Internal Revenue Service

    c. Federal Bureau of Investigation

    d. U.S. Marshals Service

9. Among other duties, the FBI has a <u>significant</u> role in

    a. investigating state fish and game licensing violations.

    b. investigating counterfeiting operations.

    c. investigating violations of the Geneva Convention.

    d. investigating terrorism.

10. Private security is associated with all of the following employment issues EXCEPT

    a. low wages.

    b. poor training.

    c. lack of standards.

    d. the inability to access private security college courses due to long waitlists and popular interest.

11. Police agencies are responsible for all of the following EXCEPT

    a. enforcing laws.

    b. providing necessary services.

    c. preventing crime.

    d. rehabilitating offenders.

76

12. In making an arrest, the most important factor for police officers is
    a. the nature of the act itself.
    b. the suspect's appearance and body language.
    c. the suspect's attitude toward authority.
    d. the suspect's criminal history.

13. The Metropolitan Police Act of 1829 was legislated in
    a. London.
    b. Paris.
    c. New York.
    d. Boston.

14. During the community era of policing, law enforcement
    a. focused heavily on reactive policing.
    b. created a number of community programs.
    c. moved away from foot patrol.
    d. emphasized impersonal public relations in order to diminish corruption.

15. In the reform-era of policing, law enforcement
    a. increased the number and types of community programs it offered.
    b. placed officers back on the foot beat.
    c. established bureaucratic operations to promote efficiency.
    d. concentrated on enhancing public relations.

16. In the political era of policing, law enforcement
    a. provided a wide range of social services to political constituents.
    b. increased training and certification standards.
    c. made use of patrol vehicles and patrol beats.
    d. emphasized higher education for officers.

17. The first state police organization was the
    a. New Mexico State Patrol.
    b. New York State Police.
    c. Massachusetts State Mounties.
    d. Texas Rangers.

18. Private security officers
    a. have full arrest powers as certified by the state in which they work.
    b. have no arrest powers at all.
    c. can make a citizen's arrest if the law permits such.
    d. are granted immunity from civil liability.

77

19. Private security is designed to
    a. deter crime.
    b. fight crime.
    c. provide services to the law enforcement community.
    d. reduce crime rates by arresting offenders.

20. Which of the following is a factor driving the growth of the private security industry?
    a. Increased fear of crime
    b. Increased professionalism in the field
    c. A shift toward service privatization by government
    d. Dissatisfaction with public police

21. Which one is NOT a reason for police officer discretion?
    a. Police officer are considered trustworthy
    b. Police officers have experience and training in their field
    c. Police officers have significant knowledge about criminal behavior
    d. Police officers are afforded discretion under article V. of the Constitution

22. U.S. Marshals
    a. provide security at federal courts.
    b. provide security for dignitaries such as the President and First Family.
    c. investigate immigration violations.
    d. protect the White House.

23. The U.S. Secret Service
    a. provides security at federal court buildings.
    b. investigates terrorism.
    c. collects terrorism related intelligence on foreign nations.
    d. combats currency counterfeiters.

24. The Wickersham Commission's findings were the prelude for the
    a. community era.
    b. political era.
    c. reform era.
    d. patronage era.

25. Which of the following is NOT the reason for police officer enforcement leniency in domestic violence service calls?
    a. Victims sometimes refuse to press criminal charges against the abusers
    b. Officers feel they are intruding in a personal family matter
    c. Making domestic violence arrests is expensive and time consuming
    d. Officers often believe that the case will not be prosecuted or that charges will most likely be 'dropped'

78

Fill in the Blank

1. Police corruption was rampant during the ___*political*___ era of policing, which lasted from 1840-1930.

2. The term "sheriff" derives from the Old English term ___*Shire reeve*___.

3. The ___*Wickersham Commission*___ of 1929 called for reform to eliminate police brutality and the corrupting influence of politics.

4. August Vollmer, a police reformer, inaugurated the first college program to grant a college degree in ___*law enforcement*___.

5. Police responsibilities include: enforcing the law, preserving the peace, ___*preventing crime*___ and providing necessary services.

6. The primary law enforcement in a county is the ___*sheriff*___.

7. Another name for medical examiner is ___*coroner*___.

8. The FBI and the U.S. Marshals Service are organized under the ___*Department of Justice*___ cabinet.

9. Police discretion is impacted by subjective factors including values, background, ___*personality*___ and beliefs.

10. U.S. Customs and Border Protection, U.S. Immigration and Customs Enforcement and the U.S. Secret Service are all organized under the ___*Dept. of Homeland Security*___ cabinet.

11. The ___*DEA*___ combats the trade of illegal drugs internationally and domestically.

12. Police departments often restrict officer ___*discretion*___ in domestic violence calls and police pursuits.

13. The ___*Dept. of Justice*___, created in 1870, is still the primary federal law enforcement agency in the country.

14. Rather than replace police officers, private security is designed to ___*deter*___ crime.

15. ___*Mandatory arrest*___ policies require that police officers must arrest a person who has battered a spouse or domestic partner.

Short Essays

1. Describe the first systems of law enforcement in colonial America.

2. Describe (tell) how the patronage system affected policing.

3. Discuss the importance of the Wickersham Commission and its results.

4. List five main types of law enforcement agencies.

5. List some of the most important law enforcement agencies under the control of the Department of Homeland Security.

6. Identify the duties of the FBI.

7. Analyze the importance of private security today.

8. List the four basic responsibilities of the police.

9. Indicate why patrol officers are allowed discretionary powers.

10. Explain how some jurisdictions have reacted to perceived leniency to perpetrators of domestic violence.

83

Answers Key

True-False:
1. T, see pg. 143, LO2
2. T, see pg. 150, LO1
3. T, see pg. 152, LO3
4. F, see pg. 150, LO1
5. T, see pg. 159, LO5
6. T, see pg. 163, LO6
7. F, see pg. 163, LO6
8. T, see pg. 165, LO6
9. T, see pg. 165, LO7
10. T, see pg. 167, LO5
11. F, see pg. 167, LO5
12. T, see pg. 171, LO8
13. F, see pg. 171, LO8
14. F, see pg. 173, LO9
15. F, see pg. 169, LO5
16. T, see pg. 174, LO10

Multiple Choice:
1. d, see pg. 149, LO1
2. d, see pg. 151, LO2
3. b, see pg. 152, LO3
4. d, see pgs. 151-154, LO3
5. a, see pg. 161, LO5
6. c, see pg. 162, LO5
7. a, see pg. 162, LO5
8. a, see pg. 163, LO6
9. d, see pg. 165, LO7
10. d, see pg. 165, LO8
11. c, see pg. 156, LO4
12. a, see pg. 174, LO9
13. a, see pg. 149, LO1
14. b, see pg. 154, LO3
15. c, see pg. 152, LO3
16. a, see pg. 151, LO2
17. d, see pg. 161, LO5
18. c, see pg. 171, LO8
19. a, see pg. 171, LO8
20. a, see pg. 172, LO8
21. d, see pg. 174, LO9
22. a, see pg. 167, LO5
23. d, see pg. 165, LO5
24. c, see pg. 152, LO3
25. c, see pg. 160, LO10

Fill in the Blank:
1. political, see pg. 151, LO2
2. shire-reeve, see pg. 150, LO1
3. Wickersham Commission, see pg.152, LO3
4. law enforcement, see pg. 152, LO3
5. preventing crime, see pg. 157, LO4
6. sheriff, see pg. 160, LO5
7. coroner, see pg. 161, LO5
8. Department of Justice, see pg. 148, LO4
9. personality, see pg. 173, LO9
10. Department of Homeland Security, see pg. 163, LO6
11. DEA, see pg. 166, LO5
12. discretion, see pg.175, LO10
13. Department of Justice, see pg. 165, LO5/6
14. deter, see pg. 171, LO8
15. mandatory arrest, see pg. 175, LO10

Short Essays:
1. See pgs. 149-152, LO1
2. See pgs. 151-152, LO2
3. See pgs. 152, LO3
4. See pg. 159, LO5
5. See pg. 163, LO6
6. See pgs. 165-166, LO7
7. See pgs. 170-172, LO8
8. See pg. 156, LO4
9. See pgs. 173-174, LO9
10. See pgs. 174-175, LO10

CHALLENGES TO EFFECTIVE POLICING

OUTLINE

Learning Objectives

After reading this chapter, you should be able to:

LO1: Identify the differences between the police academy and field training as learning tools for recruits.

LO2: Explain some of the benefits of a culturally diverse police force.

LO3: List the three primary purposes of police patrol.

LO4: Indicate some investigation strategies that are considered aggressive.

LO5: Describe how forensic experts use DNA fingerprinting to solve crimes.

LO6: Explain why differential response strategies enable police departments to respond more efficiently to 911 calls.

LO7: Explain community policing and its contribution to the concept of problem oriented policing.

LO8: Determine when police officers are justified in using deadly force.

LO9: Identify the three traditional forms of police corruption.

LO10: Explain what an ethical dilemma is and name four categories of ethical dilemmas typically facing a police officer.

Chapter Outline

I. Recruitment and Training: Becoming a Police Officer
  A. Basic Requirements
    4. U.S. citizenship
    5. No felony convictions
    6. Valid driver's license in jurisdiction
    7. 21 years of age
    8. Weight and eyesight
  B. Educational Requirements
  C. Training
    4. Academy Training
    5. In the Field Training
      a. Police recruit's training in which he or she is removed from the classroom and placed on the beat, under the supervision of a senior officer
  D. Recruiting Members of Minority Groups and Women
      a. Discrimination and the law
    1. Benefits of a culturally diverse police force
    2. Women and policing
    3. Legal discrimination
II. Police Organization
      a. Bureaucracy – a hierarchically structured administrative organization that carries out specific functions
  A. The Structure of the Police Department
    1. Delegation of Authority
      a. Hierarchy (Chain of Command)

86

B. Policy Statements: Rules for Policing
    a. Policy – set of guiding principles designed to influence the behavior and decision making of police officers

III. Law Enforcement in the Field
  A. Police on Patrol: The Backbone of the Department
    a. Sworn officer – authorized to make arrests and use force, including deadly force
    1. The Purpose of Patrol
      a. Deterrence of crime
      b. Maintenance of public order
      c. 24-hour provision of service
    2. Community Concerns
    3. Patrol Activities
      a. Preventive patrol
      b. Calls for service
      c. Administrative duties
      d. Officer-initiated activities
    4. "Noise, Booze, and Violence"
  B. Police Investigations
    a. Detective – primary police investigator of crimes
    1. Detectives in Action
    2. The Detection Function
      a. Investigators face 3 categories of cases:
        i. Unsolvable
        ii. Solvable
        iii. Already solved
  C. Aggressive Investigation Strategies
    1. Undercover
    2. Confidential Informants
      a. Human source for police who provides information concerning illegal activity in which he or she is involved
  D. Clearance Rates and Cold Cases
    1. Uncooperative Witnesses
    2. Unsolved Cases
      a. Cold cases – criminal investigation that has not been solved after a certain period of time
  E. Forensic Investigations and DNA
    a. Forensics – application of science to establish facts and evidence during the investigation of crimes
    b. Used to determine such facts as:
      i. Cause of death or injury
      ii. Time of death or injury
      iii. Type of weapon or weapons used
      iv. Identity of the offender

1. Crime Scene Forensics
    i. Trace evidence – evidence such as a fingerprint, blood, or hair found in small amounts at a crime scene
    ii. Ballistics – study of firearms, including the firing of the weapon and the flight of the bullet
    a. The Human Fingerprint
    b. Bloodstain Pattern Analysis
2. The DNA Revolution
    i. The genetic code
    ii. A wealth of evidence
    a. DNA in Action
        i. Databases and cold hits
            01. CODIS
        ii. New Developments
        iii. An Imperfect Science

IV. Police Strategies: What Works?
    A. Response Time to 911 Calls
        a. Incident-driven policing – reactive approach to policing that emphasizes a speedy response to calls for service
        1. Response Time and Efficiency
        2. Improving Response Time Efficiency
            a. Differential response – strategy for answering calls for service in which response time is adapted to the seriousness of the call
    B. Patrol Strategies
        a. General patrol
        b. Directed patrol – strategy designed to focus on a specific type of criminal activity at a specific time
        1. Testing general patrol theories in Kansas City
        2. Interpreting the Kansas City Experiment
        3. "Hot spots" and Crime Mapping
            a. Hot spot – concentrated area of criminal activity that draw a directed police response
    C. Arrest Strategies
        a. Types of Arrests:
            i. Proactive arrests – arrests that occur because of concerted efforts by law enforcement
            ii. Reactive arrests – arrests that come about as part of the ordinary routine of police patrol and responses to calls for service
        1. The Broken Windows Effect
            a. Broken Windows Theory
                i. Based on order maintenance
            b. Supporters and Critics
    D. Community Policing and Problem Solving
        a. Community policing – philosophy that emphasizes community support for and cooperation with the police in preventing crime

88

1. Return to the Community
   a. Thinking locally
2. Problem-Oriented Policing
   a. Finding a long-term solution
   b. Different terms, same approach
E. Anti-Terrorism Efforts
   1. Funds and Training
   2. Joint Operations
      a. Joint Terrorism Task Force
   3. The Homeland Security "Monster"
V. "Us versus Them": Issues in Modern Policing
   A. Police Subculture
      a. Values and perceptions that are shared by members of a police department and, to a certain extent, by all law enforcement agents
      1. Core Values of Police Subculture
         a. Socialization – process through which a police officer is taught the values and expected behavior of the police subculture
         b. Following rituals are critical:
            i. Police academy
            ii. Working with senior officer
            iii. Initial felony arrest
            iv. Use of force to make arrest
            v. Using or witnessing deadly force
            vi. Witnessing major traumatic incidents for the first time
         c. Blue curtain – term used to refer to the value placed on secrecy and the general mistrust of the outside world shared by many police officers
      2. Police Cynicism
         a. The suspicion that citizens are weak, corrupt, and dangerous
   B. The Physical and Mental Dangers of Police Work
      1. Guns and Crashes
      2. On-the-Job Pressures
   C. Authority and the Use of Force
      1. Misuse of Force
      2. The Phoenix Study
      3. Types of Force
         a. Nondeadly
         b. Deadly
            i. Reasonable force – degree of force that is appropriate to protect the police officer or other citizens and is not excessive
      4. The United States Supreme Court and Use of Force
         i. Tennessee v. Garner (1985)
      5. Less Lethal Weapons
         a. Tasers
   D. Racial and Ethnic Biases in Policing
      1. Damning Statistics

    2. Police Attitudes and Discretion

  E. Police Corruption

        a. Misuse of authority by a law enforcement officer

    1. Types of Corruption

        a. Bribery

        b. Shakedowns

        c. Mooching

    2. Corruption in the Police Subculture

  F. Police Accountability

    1. Internal Investigations

        a. Internal affairs unit – division within a police department that receives and investigates complaints of wrongdoing by police officers

    2. Citizen Oversight

        a. Process by which citizens review complaints brought against individual police officers or police departments

VI. Police Ethics

        a. Ethics – rules or standards of behavior governing a profession; aimed at ensuring the fairness and rightness of actions

  A. Ethical Dilemmas

    1. Do not know the right course of action

    2. Having difficulty doing what they consider to be right

    3. Find the wrong choice very tempting

  B. Elements of Ethics

        a. Discretion

        b. Duty

        c. Honesty

        d. Loyalty

    1. Checks for police officers:

        a. Is it legal?

        b. Is it fair?

        c. How would my family and friends feel about my decision?

        d. How does it make me feel about myself?

VII.   Criminal Justice in Action—The DNA Juggernaut

Key Terms

Ballistics (pg. 199)

Blue curtain (pg. 213)

Broken windows theory (pg. 207)

Bureaucracy (pg. 189)

Citizen oversight (pg. 221)

Clearance rate (pg. 197)

Cold case (pg.198)

Cold hit (pg.202)

Special Projects

1. Contact a local area police department (or use the Internet to locate a department that has an official website) and obtain a copy of their deadly force policy (a.k.a. use of force policy). Read the policy. Does it comply with the Supreme Court's *Tennessee v. Garner* ruling? Is the policy well written and easy to read? Document your findings in a short report.

2. Use the Internet to locate a police department that employs the community policing philosophy? How were you able to determine that they employ this philosophy? Did they identify it on their website? Is it part of the agency's mission or vision statement? In your opinion what would the average on-line visitor learn about the agency by viewing its website?

3. Using popular media, locate a recent (occurred within the last 2 years) article or news story about police corruption. Read the article and identify (1) the type of corruption and (2) the motive for the corruption, if known. What was the outcome of the corruption case? Was any official statement issued from the police department about the case? If yes, describe the statement. Lastly, was the type of corruption identified in the article discussed in your textbook?

Practice Test

True-False

_____1.   The education level (education requirements) for police entry level positions and promoted positions has been increasing.

_____2.   Courts have upheld the use of police physical agility testing where the scoring standard is the same (no preference given) for male and female candidates / employees.

_____3.   Delegation of authority means that everybody reports to the chief of police.

_____4.   Differential response is a method for prioritizing police service calls in order to handle the less complicated police service calls first.

_____5.   The Kansas City Preventive Patrol experiment proved that increasing patrols decreases crime.

_____6.   The NYPD launched CODIS, computerized mapping software, to assist with criminal investigations and track crime.

_____7.   Police patrol duties can involve crime prevention, providing services, administrative work, and self-initiated activities.

_____8.   The use of confidential informants and undercover units (to assist with criminal investigations) is considered to be an 'aggressive' investigation strategy.

_____9.   Ninety-seven percent of solvable cases are solved by detectives.

_____10.   No two people have the same genetic code.

_____11.   A metaphor used to describe the culture of police mistrust of outsiders is called the "blue curtain".

92

_____12. Grass eaters are officers who actively seek out corruption opportunities.

_____13. Reasonable force is the degree of force that is appropriate to protect the police officer or others and is never excessive.

_____14. External procedures for handling and reviewing citizen complaints can include the use of citizen oversight.

_____15. Duty is defined as the moral sense of a police officer to act in a certain manner.

_____16. Ethical dilemmas often include confusion about the right course of action and being tempted by the wrong choice.

Multiple Choice

1. Which one is NOT generally a requirement for entry level police officer employment?
   a. Be at least age 21
   b. Have earned an accredited high school diploma or its equivalent
   c. Be able to speak English and at least one non-native language
   d. Be in good physical shape relative to the position sought

2. Benefits of a culturally diverse police include all of the following EXCEPT
   a. improved community relations.
   b. higher levels of police service.
   c. better maintenance of law and order.
   d. a reduction in civil litigation.

3. As a means of delegating authority; police agencies in large cities often subdivide their jurisdiction into
   a. boroughs.
   b. beats.
   c. precincts.
   d. neighborhoods.

4. Community policing
   a. emphasizes a community service and personal engagement.
   b. emphasizes detachment to reduce the potential for police corruption.
   c. requires officers to rotate beats frequently.
   d. focuses heavily on reactive policing tactics.

5. The *broken windows* theory uses a "broken window" as a metaphor to represent the idea that
    a. residents are in control of their neighborhoods.
    b. the small problems can be overlooked in order to fix the big problems.
    c. drug violence has consumed our neighborhoods.
    d. criminal activity will be tolerated in this area.

6. Which of the following is NOT a goal of police patrol service?
    a. Patrol helps deter crime and maintain public order by the physical presence of police officers
    b. Patrol provides the public with 24-hour services, even those that are directly related to criminal activity
    c. Patrol provides the department with the opportunity to have a 100% crime enforcement rate
    d. Patrol is a means for maintaining public order and a sense of security

7. *Replication* and *matching* are stages/processes associated with
    a. fingerprint analysis.
    b. the Kansas City Preventive Patrol Study.
    c. DNA science
    d. computer mapping software that is used to analyze and attack crime in target areas.

8. Detectives should focus the majority of their time and effort on cases that
    a. are already solved but are pending criminal court actions.
    b. have low probability for being solved.
    c. have a high probability of being solved.
    d. receive a lot of media scrutiny or criticism.

9. The Village Police Department's decision to deploy extra officers to patrol the city's most dangerous and crime prone areas is an example of
    a. aggressive patrol.
    b. directed patrol.
    c. general patrol.
    d. multi-dimensional patrol.

10. Police cynicism can be described as
    a. political back scratching .
    b. the overall suspicion that citizens are weak and dangerous.
    c. mistrust of supervisors.
    d. a loss of faith in the criminal justice system.

11. Officer Scott is having a quiet shift on patrol. She decides to drive through the central business district to check on things. While inspecting the area, she observes a male suspect steal a briefcase from a parked car----this scenario is really an example of
   a. directed patrol.
   b. reactive patrol.
   c. proactive patrol.
   d. multi-dimensional patrol.

12. Generally speaking, the Internal Affairs Unit of a police department
   a. receives, reviews, and investigates complaints involving alleged police misconduct.
   b. allows citizens to have input on officer performance evaluations.
   c. is responsible for managing the recruiting and hiring process.
   d. has the authority to discipline officers up to and including termination of employment.

13. Which of the following is NOT one of the questions officers should ask of themselves when deciding whether a behavior is ethical or not?
   a. Is the behavior legal?
   b. How would my family and friends feel about my actions?
   c. Is the behavior self-promoting?
   d. How does the behavior make me feel about myself?

14. Which one is NOT usually associated with the concept of community policing?
   a. Promoting police and community partnerships
   b. Addressing the fear of crime
   c. Problem solving
   d. Reducing public corruption by keeping the police somewhat the policed

15. The text describes four categories of ethical dilemma, which of the following is NOT one of those categories?
   a. Discretion
   b. Duty
   c. Honesty
   d. Morality

16. Broken Windows Theory
   a. is based on community order maintenance.
   b. requires somewhat rigid interpersonal relations for officers.
   c. requires elaborate observation techniques and equipment.
   d. is a by-product of directed patrol.

17. General patrols
    a. are directed at hot spots.
    b. are designed to follow a circuit around a specific beat.
    c. are random in nature.
    d. allow officers to be dispatched directly from police headquarters.

18. The elements of patrol include all of the following EXCEPT
    a. crime prevention.
    b. responding to police calls for service.
    c. handling administrative duties.
    d. repairing broken or inoperable equipment on the patrol vehicle.

19. As a result of the Kansas City Preventive Patrol Experiment; an increase in the number of preventive patrols
    a. has little impact on crime or community relations.
    b. caused a significant increase in the number of crimes reported.
    c. decreased reports of crime.
    d. positively impacted community relations.

20. Which of the following was identified in the text as an *aggressive* investigation strategy?
    a. Patrol saturation
    b. Deploying officers in undercover operations
    c. Use of vehicle roadblocks
    d. Patrolling hot spots

21. Police subculture is the term used to describe
    a. the cultural diversity rate of a particular agency.
    b. the basic assumptions and values of an agency.
    c. the stress associated with the job.
    d. police corruption.

22. The "us versus them" philosophy
    a. suggests that police officers view themselves as separate from citizens.
    b. suggests that racism is a common thread in American law enforcement.
    c. eliminates justice as being a necessary part of law enforcement.
    d. is the result of years of unchecked corruption and political favoritism.

23. Identify the nickname given to corrupt police officers?
    a. Grass eaters
    b. Carnivores
    c. Moochers
    d. Badgers

96

24. Which term best describes the behavior where police officers accept free gifts (e.g., cigarettes and liquor) from citizens?
   a. Shakedown
   b. Payoff
   c. Mooching
   d. Padding

25. DNA data is indexed in
   a. AFIS.
   b. CODIS.
   c. COMPSTAT.
   d. FISA.

Fill in the Blank

1. The _____ is a controlled and militarized environment where a police recruit is first introduced to the police force.

2. A recruit's placement into a _____ program requires that the recruit train under the direction of a senior officer.

3. A business environment where formal rules govern an individual's actions and relationships to co-workers is best described as a _____.

4. Calls for service are the primary instigator of _____ policing.

5. The time lapse between the receipt of a call for service and officer arrival at the scene is known as _____ time.

6. Community policing emphasizes a partnership between _____ and community.

7. A policing philosophy requiring police to identify potential criminal activity and develop strategies to prevent or respond to that activity is called _____ policing.

8. Concentrated areas of high criminal activity and police response are known as _____.

9. _____ theory is based on "order maintenance" and strong enforcement for "quality of life" crimes.

10. The _____ patrol strategy requires that officers be designated to respond to specific activities at specific times.

97

11. A _____ is a person who is involved in criminal activity and gives information about that activity and those who engage in it to the police.

12. _____ patrol takes up approximately 40% of a patrol officer's time at work.

13. Police _____ is the suspicion that citizens are weak, corrupt, and dangerous.

14. The Supreme Court's ruling in *Tennessee v. Garner* dramatically restricted how law enforcement officers use of _____ on a fleeing suspect.

15. _____ is centered on the fundamental questions of fairness, justice, rightness, and wrongness.

16. The division of internal affairs within a police agency is responsible for investigating complaints involving alleged police _____.

Short Essays

1. Identify the differences between the police academy and field training as learning tools for recruits.

2. Explain some of the benefits of a culturally diverse police force.

3. Describe the theory behind a differential response strategy of responding to calls for service.

4. Explain community policing and its strategies.

5. Discuss the three primary purposes of patrol.

6. Discuss how forensic experts use DNA fingerprinting to solve crimes.

7. Indicate some investigation strategies that are considered aggressive.

8. Determine when police officers are justified in using deadly force.

9. Identify the three traditional forms of police corruption.

10. Explain what an ethical dilemma is and name four categories of ethical dilemmas that often face a police officer.

Answer Key

True-False:
1. T, see pg. 186, LO1
2. T, see pg. 188, LO2
3. F, see pg. 191, LO3
4. F, see pg. 204, LO6
5. F, see pg. 206, LO6
6. F, see pg. 207, LO6
7. T, see pgs. 194-195, LO3
8. T, see pg. 195, LO4
9. F, see pg. 195, LO4
10. F, see pg. 200, LO5
11. T, see pg. 213, LO9
12. F, see pg. 219, LO9
13. T, see pg. 215, LO8
14. T, see pg. 221, LO9
15. T, see pg. 223, LO10
16. T, see pg. 222, LO10

Multiple Choice:
1. c, see pg. 185, LO1
2. d, see pg. 188, LO2
3. c, see pg. 191, LO3
4. a, see pg. 208, LO7
5. d, see pgs. 207-208, LO7
6. c, see pgs. 192-193, LO3
7. c, see pg. 201, LO5
8. c, see pg. 196, LO4
9. b, see pg. 205, LO3
10. b, see pg. 213, LO9
11. b, see pg. 207, LO6
12. a, see pg. 221, LO9
13. c, see pg. 223, LO10
14. d, see pg. 223, LO7
15. d, see pg. 222, LO10
16. a, see pg. 207, LO7
17. c, see pg. 205, LO6
18. d, see pgs. 194-195, LO3
19. a, see pg. 206, LO6
20. b, see pg. 197, LO4
21. b, see pg. 208, LO9
22. a, see pg. 209, LO9
23. a, see pg. 215, LO9
24. c, see pg. 215, LO9
25. b, see pg. 198, LO5

Fill in the Blank:
1. police academy,
      see pg. 186, LO1
2. field training, see pg. 187, LO1
3. bureaucracy, see pg. 189, LO3
4. incident-driven, see pg. 204, LO6.
5. response, see pg. 204, LO6
6. police, see pg. 208, LO7
7. problem-orientated,
      see pg. 209, LO7
8. hot spots, see pg. 206, LO6
9. Broken Windows,
      see pg. 207, LO7
10. directed, see pg. 205, LO6
11. confidential informant,
      see pg. 197, LO4
12. preventive, see pg. 193, LO3
13. cynicism, see pg. 213, LO9
14. deadly force, see pg. 215, LO8
15. ethics, see pg. 222, LO10
16. misconduct or wrongdoing,
      see pg. 221, LO9

Short Essays:
1. See pgs. 186-187, LO1
2. See pgs. 187-188, LO2
3. See pgs. 204-205, LO6
4. See pgs. 207-209, LO7
5. See pgs. 192-193, LO3
6. See pgs. 199-201, LO5
7. See pgs. 196-198, LO4
8. See pgs. 215-216, LO8
9. See pgs. 219-220, LO9
10. See pgs. 222-223, LO10

CHAPTER 7

POLICE AND THE CONSTITUTION

The Rules of Law Enforcement

OUTLINE

Learning Objectives

After reading this chapter, you should be able to:

LO1: Outline the four major sources that may provide probable cause.
LO2: Explain the exclusionary rule and the exceptions to it.
LO3: Distinguish between a stop and a frisk, and indicate the importance of *Terry v. Ohio*.
LO4: List the four elements that must be present for an arrest to take place.
LO5: List the four categories of items that can be seized by use of a search warrant.
LO6: Explain when searches can be made without a warrant.
LO7: Describe the plain view doctrine and indicate one of its limitations.
LO8: Recite the *Miranda* warning.
LO9: Indicate situations in which a *Miranda* warning is unnecessary.
LO10: List the three basic types of police identification.

Chapter Outline

I. The Fourth Amendment
    a. Searches and Seizures – refers to the searching for and the confiscating of evidence by law enforcement agents
    b. Probable cause – reasonable grounds to believe the existence of facts warranting certain actions, such as the search or arrest of a person
  A. Reasonableness
  B. Probable Cause
    1. Sources of Probable Cause
      a. Personal observation
      b. Information
      c. Evidence
      d. Association
    2. The Probable Cause Framework
  C. The Exclusionary Rule
    a. Any evidence that is obtained in violation of the accused's rights under the Fourth, Fifth, and Sixth Amendments will not be admissible in criminal trial
    b. Fruit of the poisoned tree – evidence that is acquired through the use of illegally obtained evidence and is therefore inadmissible in court
    1. Establishing the Exclusionary Rule
      a. The silver platter doctrine
      b. *Rochin v. California*
        i. Shocks the conscience

2. Extending the Exclusionary Rule
   a. *Mapp v. Ohio*
3. Exceptions to the Exclusionary Rule
   a. "Inevitable discovery" – illegally obtained evidence can be admitted in court if police using lawful means would have "inevitably" discovered it
   b. "Good faith" – evidence obtained with the use of a technically invalid search warrant is admissible during trial if the police acted in good faith when they sought the warrant from a judge

II. Stops and Frisks
  A. The Elusive Definition of Reasonable Suspicion
    1. *Terry v. Ohio*
    2. The Totality of Circumstances Test
    3. Informants and Reasonable Suspicion
    4. Race and Reasonable Suspicion
      a. Racial profiling – practice of targeting members of minority groups for police stops based solely on their race, ethnicity, or national origin
  B. A Stop
    a. Brief detention of a person by law enforcement agents for questioning
  C. A Frisk
    a. Pat-down or minimal search by police to discover weapons; conducted for the purpose of protecting the officer or other citizens
    b. Not a "fishing expedition"

III. Arrests
  A. Elements of an Arrest
    1. Intent
    2. Authority
    3. Seizure or detention
    4. Understanding
  B. Arrests with a Warrant
    1. Entering a Dwelling
      a. Exigent circumstances – situations that require extralegal or exceptional actions by the police
    2. The Waiting Period
      a. Knock and announce
      b. Hudson v. Michigan
  C. Arrests without a Warrant
    a. Warrantless arrest if:
      i. Offense is committed in the presence of the officer
      ii. The officer has knowledge that a crime has been committed and probable cause to believe the crime was committed by a particular suspect

IV. Lawful Searches and Seizures
  A. The Role of Privacy in Searches

a. Privacy
b. *Katz v, United States*
   i. Two-pronged test
      01. Individual must prove that she or he expected privacy
      02. Society must recognize that expectation is reasonable
1. A Legitimate Privacy Interest
   a. *California v. Greenwood*
2. Genetic Privacy

B. Search and Seizure Warrants
1. Law enforcement officer must provide:
   a. Information showing probable cause that a crime has been or will be committed
   b. Specific information on the premises to be searched, the suspects to be found and the illegal activities taking place at those premises, and the items to be seized
2. Particularity of Search Warrants
   a. Search
   b. Seizure – the forcible taking of a person or property in response to a violation of the law
   c. Items that can be seized by search warrant:
      i. Items resulting from the crime
      ii. Items that are inherently illegal for anybody to possess
      iii. Items that can be called evidence of the crime
      iv. Items used in committing the crime
3. Reasonableness During a Search and Seizure
4. Anticipatory Search Warrants
   a. Specific evidence of a crime will be located at a named place in the future, though the evidence is not necessarily at that place when the warrant is issued

C. Searches and Seizures without Warrants
1. Searches Incidental to Arrest
2. Searches with Consent
   i. Consent voluntariness:
      01. Age, intelligence, and physical condition of the consenting suspect
      02. Any coercive behavior by the police
      03. The length of questioning and its location
   a. The Citizen's Decision
   b. The Intimidation Factor

D. Searches of Automobiles
1. Pretextual Stops
   a. *Whren v. United States*
2. Containers within a Vehicle
   a. The "Moveable Vehicle Exception"
3. Limiting Automobile Searches
   a. New York v. Belton

106

E. Plain View Doctrine
  1. 4 criteria:
     a. Item is positioned so as to be detected easily by an officer's sight or some other sense
     b. The officer is legally in a position to notice the item in question
     c. The discovery of the item is inadvertent
     d. The officer immediately recognizes the illegal nature of the item
F. Electronic Surveillance
  1. Basic Rules: Consent and Probable Cause
  2. Video and Digital Surveillance
     a. Force Multiplying
     b. Privacy Concerns
V. The Interrogation Process and *Miranda*
  A. The legal basis for *Miranda*
     1. Setting the Stage for *Miranda*
     2. The *Miranda* Case
        a. The *Miranda* rights
  B. When a *Miranda* Warning is Required
     a. Custody
  C. When a *Miranda* Warning is Not Required
     a. When police do not ask testimonial questions
     b. Police have not focused on a suspect and are questioning witnesses
     c. Person voluntarily gives information
     d. Suspect has given a private statement to another nongovernmental person
     e. During a stop and frisk, no arrest
     f. During a traffic stop
  D. The Law Enforcement Response to *Miranda*
     1. Policing Around *Miranda*
        a. Conditioning strategy
        b. De-emphasizing strategy
        c. Persuasion strategy
     2. The Problem of False Confessions
  E. The Future of *Miranda*
     1. The Erosion of *Miranda*
     2. Recording Confessions
VI. The Identification Process
  A. Essential Procedures:
     1. Showups
     2. Photo arrays
     3. Lineups
        a. Right to counsel
  B. Nontestimonial Evidence
     1. Booking
VII. Criminal Justice in Action—Racial Profiling and the Constitution

Key Terms

Affidavit (pg. 246)
Anticipatory search warrant (pg. 247)
Arrest (pg. 240)
Arrest warrant (pg. 241)
Booking (pg. 264)
Consent searches (pg. 248)
Custodial interrogation (pg. 257)
Custody (pg. 257)
Electronic surveillance (pg. 252)
Exclusionary rule (pg. 235)
Exigent circumstances (pg. 242)
Frisk (pg. 240)
Fruit of the poisoned tree (pg. 235)
"good faith" exception (pg. 236)
"inevitable discovery" exception (pg. 236)
Interrogation (pg. 256)
Miranda rights (pg. 257)
Plain view doctrine (pg. 251)
Probable cause (pg. 233)
Racial profiling (pg. 239)
Search (pg. 244)
Search warrant (pg. 245)
Searches and Seizures (pg. 234)
Searches incidental to arrest (pg. 248)
Seizure (pg. 246)
Stop (pg. 239)
Warrantless arrest (pg. 243)

Special Projects

1. Interview a patrol officer about the interview and interrogation aspect of their job. Television would have us believe that administering a suspect his or her Miranda Rights is almost an hourly occurrence. In reality, how often does a patrol officer actually administer these rights? Under what circumstances are they administered? Does it vary from what is portrayed on television? Does the officer feel that the Miranda decision has impeded police investigations?

2. On April 21, 2009, the United States Supreme Court issued an opinion significantly altering police procedure relating to the search of a motor vehicle's passenger compartment upon the arrest of an occupant. This opinion resulted from the case of _Arizona v. Gant_. Research the _Gant_ case and its updated ruling. How has the _Gant_ case affected police procedure when compared to the original controlling cases _Carroll v. United States_ and _New York v. Belton_? Compare and

contrast the cases and provide a brief overview of the legal issues in each case. Prepare a one page report on the ruling and its impact on police procedure.

3. Conduct a follow-up to question two, above. Interview a police officer about the procedural changes limiting motor vehicle searches (subsequent to driver arrest). Has the ruling changed significantly the officer's ability to enforce the law? Does the office feel that the ruling is a major obstacle? Why or why not? Has the ruling impacted departmental policies and procedures and if so how?

Practice Test

True-False

_____1.   A seizure is the forcible taking of a person or property in response to a violation of the law.

_____2.   Probable cause is any grounds to believe the existence of facts warranting an arrest.

_____3.   "Fruit of the poisoned tree" means evidence that has been acquired from other illegally obtained evidence.

_____4.   Evidence obtained through illegal means may still be admissible in court, if it is determined that the evidence in question would have been inevitably discovered anyway.

_____5.   A stop is the detention of a person for the commission of a crime.

_____6.   The "totality of circumstances" test provides leeway to law enforcement to conduct stops and investigate.

_____7.   A tip can always serve as the basis for a police stop.

_____8.   In a search, police examine a person or property to locate evidence for use in a criminal case prosecution.

_____9.   The Fourth Amendment protects people, not places.

_____10.   A search warrant affidavit is written and must be sworn in front of a person who is empowered to administer the oath.

_____11.   The plain view doctrine allows clearly visible and inadvertently discovered evidence to be seized pursuant to a lawful police investigation.

_____12. The most frequent type of warrantless search is a consent search.

_____13. Police can lawfully search garbage that has been discarded (i.e., garbage has been placed at the curb or its point of collection) without obtaining a search warrant.

_____14. "*You have the right to remain silent*" is a Constitutional right stemming from the famous *Miranda v. Arizona* case.

_____15. Under the moveable vehicle exception; law enforcement, having established probable cause to search, can in fact search any container found inside a vehicle.

_____16. The Foreign Intelligence Surveillance Act (FISA) was amended by the Patriot Act of 2001.

_____17. Line-ups and their counterpart photo arrays are both considered interrogation procedures and as such, self-incrimination protections, under the Fifth Amendment attach.

_____18. A person is in custody when they feel or believe that they are not free to leave the immediate vicinity.

_____19. Police must immediately stop questioning an in-custody suspect if that suspect invokes their right to remain silent.

_____20. Suspects have the right to be represented by counsel while standing in (participating) in a police line-up.

Multiple Choice

1. The prohibition against unreasonable search and seizure is contained within the
    a. Fourth Amendment.
    b. Fifth Amendment.
    c. Sixth Amendment.
    d. Eighth Amendment.

2. Which of the following is NOT one of the sources law enforcement would use to establish probable cause?
    a. Evidence in support of a crime
    b. Suspicion or hunch
    c. Personal observation
    d. Association

110

3. Which one is NOT an element of arrest?
   a. Intent to arrest
   b. Authority to arrest
   c. Seizure or detention
   d. Culpability

4. Which legal rule or doctrine provides a person protection from the use of illegally obtained evidence in a criminal case proceeding?
   a. Exclusionary rule
   b. Silver platter doctrine
   c. Fruit of the poisoned tree doctrine
   d. Exigent circumstances rule

5. The case of *Katz v. U.S.* established the standard for
   a. conducting strip searches.
   b. a reasonable expectation of privacy.
   c. the arrest of fleeing felons.
   d. conducting electronic surveillance.

6. A search warrant must
   a. be based on probable cause.
   b. be based on reasonable suspicion.
   c. contain the names of informants who provided information leading to the desired search.
   d. be issued after a suspect has been identified and arrested.

7. The categories of items subject to seizure under a valid search warrant include all of the following EXCEPT
   a. stolen goods or instruments of crime.
   b. items that are inherently illegal (contraband).
   c. items identified as "evidence" of a crime.
   d. items not specifically identified in the warrant and are otherwise not readily identifiable as evidence or contraband.

8. The most frequently used exception to the search warrant requirement is the
   a. search incidental to arrest.
   b. consent search.
   c. plain view search.
   d. exigent circumstances search.

9. The *Miranda* rights are required
   a. at the time a suspect is arrested.
   b. at the time a suspect is booked.
   c. immediately preceding custodial interrogation of a suspect.
   d. at the onset of a stop and frisk investigation of a suspect.

10. Inherent coercion occurs when
    a. a suspect confesses but later recants the confession.
    b. DNA evidence exculpates the suspect.
    c. a technical error invalidates a previously valid search warrant.
    d. the atmosphere of an interrogation is in itself coercive.

11. Which one is NOT a police procedural method for suspect identification?
    a. Photo array
    b. Line-up
    c. Show-up
    d. Suspect booking records

12. The Fourth Amendment affirms (protects) the rights of
    a. persons.
    b. houses.
    c. papers.
    d. places.

13. Evidence obtained pursuant to an executed search warrant that was later ruled "technically invalid," may be admissible in court under an exception to the *exclusionary rule* known as
    a. inevitable discovery.
    b. officer certainty.
    c. good faith exception.
    d. the silver platter doctrine.

14. During a frisk, a police officer is permitted to search for
    a. a suspect's identification.
    b. contraband.
    c. dangerous weapons.
    d. drugs.

15. Which one does NOT rise to the level of exigent circumstances for the purposes of conducting a warrantless search?
    a. A suspect poses a strong threat of violence
    b. Persons in a residential dwelling are actively destroying evidence
    c. Officers can see or hear an in-progress assault crime inside of a residence
    d. Nightfall is starting to set in over an outdoor wooded crime scene; if officers wait for the search warrant to be issued; search capabilities will be severely impacted

16. When an officer downplays the significance of *Miranda* in order to convince a suspect to waive rights, the officer is
      a. using a conditioning technique.
      b. using a deemphasizing technique.
      c. using a persuasion technique.
      d. using inherent coercion.

17. Officer Scott is preparing a search warrant for a judge to review. Officer Scott must identify the type of items that she hopes to seize (pursuant to the warrant) by particularly describing them on the
      a. search warrant.
      b. affidavit.
      c. deposition.
      d. report.

18. When officers are searching a suspect incidental to arrest, they must limit the scope of their search to
      a. only the suspect's person.
      b. only the structure where the suspect was arrested.
      c. only the suspect's person and his/her vehicle.
      d. only the suspect's person and the area within the suspect's immediate control.

19. The "movable vehicle" exception to the Fourth Amendment was established by Supreme Court ruling in which case?
      a. *Wren v. United States*
      b. *Chimel v. California*
      c. *Carroll v. United States*
      d. *Maryland v. Wilson*

20. Plainview is
      a. an exception to the search warrant requirement.
      b. only applicable to the states.
      c. only applicable to federal officers.
      d. a direct violation of the Fourth Amendment.

21. The *Miranda* warning includes all of the following EXCEPT
      a. the right to remain silent.
      b. the right to privacy of thought.
      c. the right to have counsel appointed if indigent.
      d. the right to consult counsel before and during questioning.

22. *Miranda* is a direct result of the
    a. Fourth Amendment.
    b. Fifth Amendment.
    c. Sixth Amendment.
    d. Eighth Amendment.

23. Which scenario requires the *Miranda* warning to be administered?
    a. A suspect volunteers information about a crime to a police officer
    b. At the start of the booking procedure question and answer process
    c. During a traffic investigation (traffic stop) where there is no arrest
    d. At the start of a custodial interrogation

24. According to Professor Rolando v. del Carmen; the elements of arrest include
    a. intent.
    b. means.
    c. motive.
    d. ability.

25. A search warrant authorizing electronic surveillance must
    a. detail with "particularity" the conversations to be heard.
    b. identify the language spoken in the conversations to be heard.
    c. outline with detail how the conversation to be heard rises to the level of a national security threat.
    d. identify at least one consensual party to the conversation to be heard.

Fill in the Blank

1. The likelihood that a crime was committed and the suspect in question committed that crime is sufficient to establish _____.

2. The _____ rule directly relates to evidence seized in violation of the Fourth, Fifth, or Sixth Amendments.

3. Evidence seized pursuant to search warrant that was later ruled to be *technically invalid* may still be used in a criminal case proceeding under the _____ exception.

4. If an officer believes a person is armed, the officer may pat down the person's outer clothing to search for _____.

5. The precedent for the ever-elusive definition of _____ was finally established in the case of *Terry v. Ohio*.

6. A written order, based on probable cause and issued by a judge or magistrate, commanding that a person be arrested by the police is known as a(n) _____.

7. Once an arrest is made, the arresting officer must prove to a judge that _____ existed.

8. When reasonable suspicion exists, police officers are well within their rights to _____ and _____ a suspect.

9. The warrantless search of an arrested suspect and the area within that suspect's immediate control is known as search _____ to arrest.

10. The Patriot Act amended the _____ Act by eliminating the probable cause requirement for procuring electronic surveillance to gather foreign intelligence provided that the action serves a "significant purpose".

11. Direct questioning of a suspect to gather evidence of criminal activity and to try to gain a confession is _____.

12. Plain view requires that a police officer be _____ in a position to notice the item in question.

13. When police show pictures of potential suspects to a witness, they are using a _____ to try and secure a suspect identification.

14. During the _____ process, a police officer records an arrested suspect's name, offense type, address, and physical description into a police log/database.

15. A _____ is the brief detention of a suspect for the purpose of questioning that suspect.

Short Essays

1. Outline the four major sources that may provide probable cause.

2. Explain the exclusionary rule and the exceptions to it.

3. Distinguish between a stop and a frisk, and indicate the importance of *Terry v. Ohio*.

4. List the four elements that must be present for an arrest to take place.

5. List the four categories of items that can be seized by use of a search warrant.

6. Explain when searches can be made without a warrant.

7. Describe how the Patriot Act changed the guidelines for electronic surveillance of suspected terrorists.

8. Recite the *Miranda* warning.

9. Indicate situations in which a *Miranda* warning is unnecessary.

10. List the three basic types of police identification processes.

Answer Key

True-False:
1. T, see pg. 246, LO6
2. F, see pg. 233, LO1
3. T, see pg. 235, LO2
4. T, see pg. 236, LO2
5. F, see pg. 239, LO3
6. T, see pg. 238, LO3
7. F, see pg. 238, LO3
8. T, see pg. 244, LO5
9. T, see pg. 244, LO5
10. T, see pg. 246, LO5
11. T, see pg. 251, LO7
12. F, see pg. 248, LO6
13. T, see pg. 244, LO6
14. T, see pg. 256, LO8
15. F, see pg. 250, LO6
16. T, see pg. 251, LO6
17. T, see pg. 263, LO10
18. T, see pg. 257, LO8
19. T, see pg. 259, LO9
20. T, see pg. 263, LO10

Multiple Choice:
1. a, see pg. 233, LO1
2. b, see pg. 234, LO1
3. d, see pg. 237, LO4
4. a, see pg. 235, LO2
5. b, see pg. 244, LO5
6. a, see pg. 245, LO5
7. d, see pg. 246, LO5
8. a, see pg. 248, LO6
9. c, see pg. 257, LO9
10. d, see pg. 257, LO9
11. d, see pg. 263, LO10
12. a, see pg. 244, LO5
13. c, see pg. 236, LO2
14. c, see pg. 240, LO3
15. d, see pg. 242, LO6
16. b, see pg. 259, LO9
17. b, see pg. 246, LO5
18. d, see pg. 248, LO6
19. c, see pg. 249, LO6
20. a, see pg. 251, LO7
21. b, see pg. 256, LO8
22. b, see pg. 256, LO8
23. d, see pg. 257, LO9
24. a, see pg. 241, LO4
25. a, see pg. 252, LO6

Fill in the Blank:
1. probable cause, see pg. 233, LO1
2. exclusionary, see pg. 235, LO2
3. good faith, see pg. 236, LO2
4. weapons, see pg. 240, LO3
5. reasonable suspicion, see pg. 237, LO3
6. arrest warrant, see pg. 241, LO4
7. probable cause, see pg. 235, LO/4
8. stop, frisk, see pg. 237, LO3
9. incidental, see pg. 248, LO6
10. FISA, see pg. 253, LO6.
11. interrogation, see pg. 256, LO9
12. legally, see pg. 251, LO7.
13. photo array, see pg. 263, LO10
14. booking, see pg. 264, LO9
15. stop, see pg. 240, LO3

Short Essays:
1. See pg. 234, LO1
2. See pgs. 235-236, LO2
3. See pgs. 237-240, LO3
4. See pg. 241, LO4
5. See pg. 246, LO5
6. See pgs. 247-252, LO6
7. See pg. 251, LO7
8. See pg. 256, LO8
9. See pgs. 257-258, LO9
10. See pg. 263, LO10

COURTS AND THE QUEST FOR JUSTICE

OUTLINE

Learning Objectives

After reading this chapter, you should be able to:

LO1: Define and contrast the four functions of the courts.
LO2: Define jurisdiction and contrast geographical and subject-matter jurisdiction.
LO3: Explain the difference between trial and appellate courts.
LO4: Outline the several levels of a typical state court system.
LO5: Outline the federal court system.
LO6: Explain briefly how a case is brought to the Supreme Court.
LO7: List the actions that a judge might take prior to an actual trial.
LO8: Explain the difference between the selection of judges at the state level and at the federal level.
LO9: List and describe the members of the courtroom work group.
LO10: Explain the consequences of excessive caseloads.

Chapter Outline

I. Functions of the Courts
    1. Provides an environment in which the basis of argument can be decided through the application of law
    2. Court's legitimacy (impartiality and independence) must be unquestioned
    A. Due Process and Crime Control in the Courts
        1. The Due Process Function
            a. Protecting the rights of individuals against the power of the state
        2. The Crime Control Function
            a. Emphasizes punishment and retribution
    B. The Rehabilitation Function
        1. Based on Medical model:
            a. Criminals are patients and courts are physicians
    C. The Bureaucratic Function
        1. Court concerned with speed and efficiency
II. The Basic Principles of the American Judicial System
    1. 52 separate systems:
        a. 50 states
        b. District of Columbia
        c. Federal
    A. Jurisdiction
        a. To speak the law
    B. Geographical Jurisdiction
        a. Determined by legislation
        b. Federal versus state jurisdiction

122

        i.   Crime considered a state and local issue
        ii. Concurrent jurisdiction
           01. Two different court systems have simultaneous jurisdiction
    c. State versus State Jurisdiction
        i.   Extradition – formal process by which one legal authority
           transfers a fugitive to another legal authority
    d. Multiple Trials
  2. International Jurisdiction
    a. Extradition Treaties
    b. The Long Arm of the Law
        i.   Anti-terrorism laws
        ii. PROTECT – sex with minor
  3. Subject-Matter Jurisdiction
    a. General jurisdiction courts
    b. Limited jurisdiction courts
C. Trial and Appellate Courts
  1. Trial courts have original jurisdiction, courts of first instance
  2. Appellate courts – reviewing courts
D. The Dual Court System
  1. Supreme Court can hear cases from federal and state level
  2. Federal and state courts both have limited jurisdiction
III. State Court Systems
  1. Can include:
    a. Lower courts
    b. Trial courts
    c. Appellate courts
    d. State's highest court
A. Courts of Limited Jurisdiction
  1. Magistrate Courts
    a. Presided by justice of the peace
  2. Specialty Courts
    a. Drug court
    b. Gun court
    c. Juvenile court
    d. Domestic court
    e. Elder court
B. Trial Courts of General Jurisdiction
C. State Courts of Appeals
IV. The Federal Court System
  1. Judges appointed for life
A. U.S. District Courts
  1. Lowest tier
  2. 94 districts
B. U.S. Courts of Appeal
  1. 13 U.S. Courts of Appeals
C. U.S. Supreme Court

    a. Neither power of purse or sword
1. Interpreting and Applying the Law
    a. Judicial Review – power of court to determine whether a law or action by the other branches is constitutional
    b. Statutory Interpretation – must determine the meaning of certain statutory provisions when applied to specific situations
2. Jurisdiction of the Supreme Court
    a. Nine justices
    b. Most work is appellate
3. Which Cases Reach the Supreme Court?
    a. Writ of Certiorari – orders lower court to send record of case for review
    b. Court will not issue a writ unless at least 4 justices approve – rule of four
4. Supreme Court Decisions
        i. Attorneys present oral arguments
    b. Concurring opinions
    c. Dissenting opinions
V. Judges in the Court System
    A. The Roles and Responsibilities of Trial Judges
        1. Before the Trial
            a. Sufficient probable cause to issue a search or arrest warrant
            b. Sufficient probable cause to authorize electronic surveillance
            c. Enough evidence to justify temporary incarceration
            d. Should defendant be released on bail
            e. Accept pretrial motions
            f. Accept plea bargain
        2. During the Trial
            a. Referee
            b. Teacher
        3. The Administrative Role
            a. Docket or calendar of cases
    B. Selection of Judges
            a. Independence
            b. Accountability
        1. Appointment of Judges
            a. Problem of Patronage
        2. Election of Judges
            a. Partisan
            b. Non-partisan
        3. Merit Selection
            a. Missouri Plan
    C. Diversity on the Bench
    D. The Impact of Past Discrimination
        1. The Benefits of Diversity
    E. Judicial Conduct

124

1. Judicial Ethics
   a. ABA Model Code of Judicial Conduct
   b. Judicial Misconduct
2. The Recusal Requirement
   a. Judge has personal bias or prejudice concerning one of the parties to the trial
   b. Judge served as a lawyer or worked as a government employee on the matter
   c. Judge has financial or other interest in subject matter
   d. Judge or family member is likely to called as a witness
3. The Removal of Judges
   a. Impeachment
VI. The Courtroom Work Group
   A. Members of the Group
      1. Judge, Prosecutor, Defense Attorney
      2. Bailiff
      3. Clerk of the Court
      4. Court Reporter
   B. Formation of the Courtroom Work Group
   C. The Judge in the Courtroom Work Group
   D. Assembly Line Justice
      a. Sacrificed justice for efficiency
      1. The Impact of Excessive Caseloads
      2. The Courtroom Work Group and Overloaded Courts
VII. Criminal Justice in Action—The International Criminal Court

Key Terms

Appellate courts (pg. 279)
Concurrent jurisdiction (pg. 275)
Concurring opinions (pg. 286)
Courtroom work group (pg. 295)
Dissenting opinions (pg. 286)
Docket (pg. 288)
Dual Court System (pg. 279)
Extradition (pg. 277)
Impeach (pg. 294)
Judicial misconduct (pg. 293)
Judicial review (pg. 284)
Jurisdiction (pg. 275)
Magistrate (pg. 281)
Missouri Plan (pg. 290)
Nonpartisan elections (pg. 288)
Opinions (pg. 279)
Oral arguments (pg. 285)

Partisan elections (pg. 288)
Recusal (pg. 293)
Rule of four (pg. 285)
Specialty Courts (pg. 281)
Trial Courts (pg. 278)
Writ of certiorari (pg. 285)

Special Projects

1. Visit a courtroom on a day when proceedings are being held. Observe the proceedings and take some notes. Identify at least two of the proceedings and detail your observations. Were you able to follow the proceedings? Were they confusing? Were you surprised by any of the activities? Did it appear to be an organized operation? Did your impression of the justice system change?

2. Using the Internet, research a criminal court case that has had at least one appeal. What was the basis for the appeal? Identify the court of original jurisdiction. What was the conclusion to the case (if known)? If the case is still being decided, what do you think might happen?

3. Using popular media and/or the Internet to conduct some research to locate a case involving judicial misconduct. Identify (1) the misconduct, (2) the impact that the misconduct had on the case, (3) the jurisdiction, (4) judicial sanctions, if known, and (5) how the judge came to be seated (election or appointment). What is your opinion of the case and its outcome? What do you think should happen to the judge?

Practice Test

True-False

_____1.   The primary concern of early American courts was to protect the rights of the individual against the vast power of the state.

_____2.   The court's bureaucratic function is to keep the justice process moving along.

_____3.   An opinion is a statement by a judge or Justice expressing personal beliefs as the basis for a case ruling or decision.

_____4.   Magistrates have jurisdiction to issue search warrants.

_____ 5.   State trial courts with general jurisdiction may also be known as county courts, district courts, superior courts, or circuit courts.

_____ 6.   Every state has at least one court of appeals.

_____ 7.   The U.S. Supreme Court is comprised of seven Justices and a Chief Justice.

_____ 8.   The Rule of Four requires that a minimum of four Supreme Court Justices make any decision.

_____ 9.   Arguments that erupt spontaneously during a criminal court proceeding are better known as "oral arguments."

_____ 10.   The judge is both a teacher and a referee during a trial.

_____ 11.   With regard to the judicial selection process; the two key concepts that are often intensely debated are (1) independence and (2) accountability.

_____ 12.   In a non-partisan election, candidates are identified by name and political party affiliation.

_____ 13.   In a partisan election, candidates openly receive support from political parties.

_____ 14.   Elder courts are considered "specialty courts" and they focus primarily on the special needs of the elderly victims rather than elderly offenders.

_____ 15.   The ABA's Code of Judicial Conduct is a binding document.

_____ 16.   The relationships among the courtroom work group have a far-reaching impact on the day-to-day operation of the court.

_____ 17.   The court clerk is responsible for supervising the jury during the deliberation process.

_____ 18.   The court reporter is responsible for publishing court rulings to the ABA and the local state bar association.

Multiple Choice

1. The primary underlying values of the criminal justice system are
    a. the protection of citizens and the state.
    b. enforcing and supporting the law.
    c. due process and crime control.
    d. rehabilitating and mentoring criminal offenders.

2. The crime control function of the court emphasizes
    a. deterrence.
    b. retribution.
    c. rehabilitation.
    d. incapacitation.

3. The courts' need for speed and efficiency is addressed by its
    a. due process function.
    b. crime control function.
    c. rehabilitation function.
    d. bureaucratic function.

4. Which term best describes an occasion where two different courts have jurisdiction over the same matter?
    a. Dual court system
    b. General jurisdiction
    c. Concurrent jurisdiction
    d. Double jeopardy

5. Lower courts that manage misdemeanor cases are better known as
    a. courts of general jurisdiction.
    b. appellate courts.
    c. courts of limited jurisdiction.
    d. specialty courts.

6. The federal court system includes
    a. U.S. district courts.
    b. U.S. county courts.
    c. U.S. superior courts.
    d. U.S. magistrate courts

7. Which of the following best describes "concurring opinions"?
    a. Opinions prepared by individual members of the Supreme Court in support of the Court's ruling.
    b. Any Supreme Court opinion not authored by the Chief Justice.
    c. Opinions that may voice disapproval of the grounds on which a decision was made.
    d. Opinions that support a Supreme Court ruling but are authored by bar members not directly related to the case as part of amicus.

8. Which one is NOT a pretrial activity or action?
    a. A hearing to determine if there exists sufficient probable cause to take the case to trial
    b. Bail setting
    c. Plea bargaining or review of alternative sentences
    d. Jury deliberations

9. In the Missouri Plan, judges
    a. must be both appointed and elected.
    b. are chosen by way of public partisan election.
    c. are appointed by senate committee.
    d. are chosen by seniority (as a practicing lawyer).

10. Which of the following is NOT associated with the concept of judicial misconduct?
    a. Diminished public confidence in the court system
    b. Bribery and corruption.
    c. The appearance of impropriety
    d. Diversity on the bench

11. How is a judge officially come to be recused from a proceeding?
    a. The prosecutor officially affirms the recusal
    b. The judge is responsible to recuse himself (herself)
    c. The ABA affirms all recusal actions
    d. The defense attorney officially affirms the recusal

12. The clerk of the court
    a. maintains all paperwork associated with the trial/proceeding.
    b. records all that is said during proceedings.
    c. decides what proposed matter(s) will be acted upon by the judge.
    d. delivers summonses.

13. The dual court system
    a. allows celebrity trials to be tried in any jurisdiction.
    b. cannot accommodate civil cases.
    c. includes both state and federal courts.
    d. allows judges the opportunity to laterally transfer between state and federal seats.

14. Courts of limited jurisdiction would most likely hear cases involving
    a. an appeal of a lower court's ruling.
    b. felony cases.
    c. traffic violations and other minor offenses.
    d. only labor law disputes.

15. Specialty courts include all of the following EXCEPT
    a. gun court.
    b. juvenile court.
    c. domestic court.
    d. civil court.

16. How many United States Courts of Appeal are there?
    a. Nine
    b. Thirteen
    c. Eleven
    d. Seven

17. How many Justices (including the Chief Justice) serve on the United States Supreme Court?
    a. Nine
    b. Eight
    c. Twelve
    d. Seven

18. Which one is not considered to be the judge's responsibility during a trial?
    a. Ensuring that proper procedures are followed during jury selection
    b. Explaining points of law as needed
    c. Officiating over the proceedings
    d. Filing motions for action or inaction

19. When it comes to selecting a judge, which of the following is considered to be fundamental?
    a. Magna cum laude honors
    b. Trial experience
    c. Independence
    d. Service to the ABA

20. When judicial candidates align themselves with a particular political party, they are seeking election to public office by way of
      a. partisan public election.
      b. the Scott plan.
      c. the Missouri Plan.
      d. non-partisan public election.

21. How many African American Justices have been confirmed to the United States Supreme Court?
      a. One
      b. Two
      c. Three
      d. None

22. Which one is NOT a problem or consequence (identified in the text) as being associated with "assembly line justice"?
      a. Sacrifice of justice
      b. Unsatisfactory plea bargains
      c. Early release of dangerous offenders
      d. Unnecessary or extended incarceration

23. How many female Justices have been confirmed to the United States Supreme Court?
      a. One
      b. Two
      c. Three
      d. Four

24. In the federal court system, judges are selected by
      a. public election.
      b. a vote of their judicial peers.
      c. Presidential appointment and senate confirmation.
      d. tenure and senate confirmation.

25. U.S. Supreme Court rulings are decided in
      a. oral arguments.
      b. briefs.
      c. closed sessions.
      d. conferences.

Fill in the Blank

1. A _____ is a place where legal arguments are settled through the application of law.

2. The rehabilitation function of the court is based on the _____ model.

3. Jurisdiction is the _____ of the court.

4. Courts that handle limited subject matter cases are called courts of _____.

5. Elder courts, gun courts, and drug courts are have narrow jurisdiction and as such are classified as _____ courts.

6. The process of _____ involves one jurisdiction surrendering an accused offender to another jurisdiction for prosecution.

7. Courts that review decisions made by trial courts are _____ courts.

8. The United States is recognized as a _____ court system because it is made up of both state and federal courts.

9. A _____ is a request issued to a lower court demanding that it send a specific case record to the Supreme Court for review.

10. When a Supreme Court Justice expresses written disagreement about a decision made by a fellow Justice, this is known as a _____ opinion.

11. The _____ is essentially a list of scheduled court cases.

12. The _____ if responsible for courtroom security.

13. Judicial selection often focuses on a candidate's ability to be _____.

14. One of the main criticisms levied against the American court system is that it has sacrificed _____ for efficiency.

Short Essays

1. Define and contrast the four functions of the courts.

2. Define jurisdiction and contrast geographical and subject-matter jurisdiction.

3. Explain the difference between trial and appellate courts.

4. Outline the several levels of a typical state court system.

5. Outline the federal court system.

6. Explain briefly how a case is brought to the Supreme Court.

7. List the actions that a judge might take prior to an actual trial.

8. Explain the difference between the selection of judges at the state level and at the federal level.

9. List and describe the members of the courtroom work group.

10. Explain the consequences of excessive caseloads.

Answer Key

True-False:
1. T, see pg. 273, LO1
2. T, see pg. 274, LO1
3. F, see pg. 279, LO3
4. T, see pg. 280, LO4
5. T, see pg. 282, LO4
6. T, see pg. 282, LO4
7. F, see pg. 285, LO5
8. F, see pg. 285, LO6
9. F, see pg. 285, LO6
10. T, see pgs. 287-288, LO7
11. T, see pg. 290, LO8
12. F, see pg. 288, LO8
13. T, see pg. 288, LO8
14. T, see pg. 282, LO4
15. F, see pg. 294, LO9
16. T, see pg. 296, LO9
17. F, see pg. 296, LO9
18. F, see pg. 296, LO9

Multiple Choice:
1. c, see pg. 273, LO1
2. b, see pg. 274, LO1
3. d, see pg. 274, LO1
4. c, see pg. 275, LO2
5. c, see pg. 280, LO3
6. a, see pg. 283, LO5
7. a, see pg. 286, LO6
8. d, see pg. 287, LO7
9. a, see pg. 290, LO8
10. d, see pg. 293, LO8
11. b, see pg. 293, LO8
12. a, see pg. 296, LO9
13. c, see pg. 279, LO3
14. c, see pg. 281, LO4
15. d, see pgs. 281-282, LO4
16. b, see pg. 283, LO5
17. a, see pg. 285, LO5
18. d, see pg. 287. LO7
19. c, see pg. 288, LO8
20. a, see pg. 288, LO8
21. b, see pg. 291, LO8
22. d, see pg. 299, LO10
23. c, see pg. 292, LO8
24. c, see pg. 289, LO8
25. d, see pg. 285, LO6

Fill in the Blank:
1. court, see pg. 273, LO1
2. medical model, see p. 274, LO1
3. authority, see pg. 275, LO2
4. limited jurisdiction, see pg. 280, LO4
5. specialty, see pgs. 281-282, LO4
6. extradition, see pg. 277, LO2
7. appellate, see pg. 279, LO3
8. dual, see pg. 279, LO3/4
9. writ of *certiorari*, see pg. 285, LO6
10. dissenting, see pg. 286, LO6
11. docket, see pg. 288, LO4
12. bailiff, see pg. 296, LO9
13. independent, see pg. 288, LO8
14. justice, see pg. 299, LO10

Short Essays:
1. See pgs. 273-274, LO1
2. See pgs. 275-278, LO2
3. See pgs. 278-279, LO3
4. See pgs. 280-282, LO4
5. See pgs. 283-286, LO5
6. See pg. 285, LO6
7. See pg. 287, LO7.
8. See pgs. 288-290, LO8
9. See pg. 296, LO9
10. See pgs. 299-300, LO10

CHAPTER 9

PRETRIAL PROCEDURES

The Adversary System in Action

OUTLINE

Learning Objectives

After reading this chapter, you should be able to:

LO1: List the different names given to public prosecutors and the general powers that they have.

LO2: Contrast the prosecutor's role as an elected official and as a crime fighter.

LO3: Delineate the responsibilities of defense attorneys.

LO4: Indicate the three types of defense allocation programs.

LO5: List the three basic features of an adversary system of justice.

LO6: Identify the steps involved in the pretrial criminal process.

LO7: Indicate the three influences on a judge's decision to set bail.

LO8: Explain how a prosecutor screens potential cases.

LO9: List and briefly explain the different forms of plea bargaining agreements.

LO10: Indicate the ways that both defense attorneys and prosecutors can induce plea bargaining.

Chapter Outline

I.   The Prosecution
1.   Criminal cases are tried by public prosecutors
a.   In federal system known as U.S attorney
b.   In state and local courts known as:
i.   Prosecuting attorney
ii. State prosecutor
iii. District attorney
iv. County attorney
v.   City attorney
A.   Office of the Prosecutor
1.   Officer of the Law
a.   Has great deal of discretion in:
i.   Whether an individual arrested by the police will be charged with a crime
ii. The level of charges to be brought against the suspect
iii. If and when to stop prosecution
2.   Special Prosecution
a.   Narcotic or gang crimes
B.   The Prosecutor as an Elected Official
1.   Community Pressures
a.   Must answer to the voters
C.   The Prosecutor as Crime Fighter
1.   Police-Prosecutor Conflict
a.   Attributed to different backgrounds
i.   Prosecutors from middle or upper-class
ii. Police from working class

138

        b. Basic divergence in the concept of guilt
            i. Police-factual guilt
            ii. Prosecutors-legal guilt
    2. Attempts at Cooperation
        a. Improving communication
II. The Defense Attorney
    A. The Responsibilities of the Defense Attorney
        1. Representing the defendant during custodial process:
            a. Arrest
            b. Interrogation
            c. Lineup
            d. Arraignment
        2. Investigating the incident
        3. Communication with prosecutor
        4. Preparing for trial
        5. Submitting motions
        6. Representing at trial
        7. Negotiating a sentence
        8. Appeal
    B. Defending the Guilty
    C. The Public Defender
        1. Two types:
            a. Private Attorneys
            b. Public defenders
                i. *Gideon v. Wainwright*
                ii. *In re Gault*
                iii. *Argersinger v. Hamlin*
        2. Eligibility Issues
            a. Varies by jurisdiction
        3. Defense Counsel Programs:
            a. Assigned Counsel
            b. Contracting Attorney Programs
            c. Public Defender Programs
    D. Effectiveness of Public Defenders
        a. Conviction rates of defendants with private counsel and those with public defenders are generally the same
        1. Unreasonable Caseloads
        2. Unreasonable Pay
        3. The Strickland Standard
            a. *Strickland v. Washington*
                i. Attorney's performance was deficient
                ii. Deficiency more likely than not caused the defendant to lose the case
    E. The Attorney-Client Relationship
        1. Relationships between public defenders and clients often marred by suspicion on both sides

139

F. Attorney-Client Privilege
    a. Communication between client and attorney be kept confidential
    1. The Privilege and Confessions
    2. The Exception to the Privilege
        a. *U.S. v. Zolin*
           i. Lawyers may disclose contents of conversation concerning a crime that has yet to be committed
III. Truth, Victory, and the Adversary System
  A. Three Features:
    1. Neutral and passive decision makers (judge or jury)
    2. Presentation of evidence by prosecution and defense
    3. Structured procedure to be followed
IV. Pretrial Detention
  A. Initial appearance – must occur promptly
    1. Defendant informed of charges
    2. Explains constitutional rights
    3. Attorney appointed
  B. The Purpose of Bail
    1. Provided for under 8th Amendment
    2. Protect the community from another crime before trial
  C. Setting Bail
    a. Determined by jurisdiction
    1. The Judge and Bail Setting – influencing factors:
        a. Uncertainty of information about defendant
        b. Risk of releasing defendant
        c. Overcrowded jails
    2. Prosecutors, Defense Attorneys, and Bail Setting
        a. May influence judge's decision
  D. Gaining Pretrial Release
    1. Release on Recognizance
        a. Judge determines defendant is not at risk to jump bail and does not pose a threat to community
    2. Posting Bail
        a. Felons rarely released on recognizance
        b. Property bonds – property valued at double the bail amount
    3. Bail Bondspersons
        a. Promises the court that defendant will show for trial or they will pay full amount
        b. Ten percent cash bail – court accepts deposit of 10% of full amount
  E. Preventive Detention
    1. Allows judges to deny bail to suspects with prior records or violence or nonappearance
    2. Upheld by U.S. Supreme Court in *U.S. v. Salerno*
V. Establishing Probable Cause
    1. Crime was committed and link defendant to crime
  A. The Preliminary Hearing

140

      a. Judge or magistrate decides whether evidence presented is sufficient for the case to proceed to trial

      b. Held no later than 10 days

   1. The Preliminary Hearing Process

      a. Conducted like a mini-trial

      b. Defense starts process of *discovery*:

         i. Entitled to access to any evidence prosecutor has

         ii. Keystone of adversary process

   2. Waiving the Hearing

      a. Grand jury – indictment

      b. Prosecutor - information

  B. The Grand Jury

      a. Group of citizens called to decide whether probable cause exists

         i. Impaneled

   1. The "Shield" and the "Sword"

      a. Shields individual from power of the state

      b. Opportunity for government to provide evidence against the accused - sword

   2. A "Rubber Stamp"

      a. Defendants indicted at a rate of 99%

VI. The Prosecutorial Screening Process

   1. Once police have initially charged the defendant prosecutor can prosecute the case, reduce or increase the initial charge, file additional charges or dismiss the case

  A. Case Attrition

      a. Fewer than 1 in 3 adults arrested for a felony see the inside of a prison cell

   1. Scarce Resources

      a. About ½ of adult felony cases brought to prosecutors are dismissed through *nolle prosequi* (unwilling to pursue)

   2. Screening Factors

      a. Sufficient evidence for conviction

      b. Case priorities

      c. Uncooperative victims

      d. Unreliability of victims

      e. Defendant willing to testify against others

  B. Prosecutorial Charging and the Defense Attorney

   1. Pretrial motions:

      a. Suppress illegally obtained evidence

      b. Change of venue

      c. Invalidate search warrant

      d. Dismiss for delay

      e. Obtain prosecutorial evidence

VII. Pleading Guilty

   1. Nolo contendere

      a. I will not contest it

A. Plea Bargaining in the Criminal Justice System
    1. Normally after arraignment
        a. Charge bargaining
        b. Sentence bargaining
        c. Count bargaining
B. Motivation for Plea Bargaining
    1. Prosecutors and Plea Bargaining
        a. Conviction
    2. Defense Attorneys and Plea Bargaining
        a. Best defense
    3. Defendants and Plea Bargaining
        a. Measure of control
    4. Victims and Plea Bargaining
        a. Voice in outcome
C. Plea Bargaining and the Adversary System
    1. Strategies to Induce a Plea Bargain
        a. Lack of a strong case
        b. Overcharging
            i. Horizontal and vertical
    2. Protecting the Defendant
        a. *Boykin* form
VIII. Going to Trial

Key Terms

Special Projects

1. Identify a criminal case that received a fair amount of media scrutiny because it was adjudicated by way of a plea bargain. What was the theme of the negative publicity? Was it directed at the police, the prosecutor, or the judge? Did the terms of the plea bargain or case disposition vary drastically from other similar cases? Did the publicity change the outcome of the case or cause someone to offer a public explanation as to the circumstances of the deal?

2. Conduct some research to determine whether or not your state requires the grand jury process as part of the pretrial procedure. In either case write a short report on your state's pretrial procedure (i.e., grand jury or preliminary examination). Do you think that this pretrial process is necessary?

3. Interview an attorney about the attorney-client privilege rule. Has the attorney ever felt compelled to breech it, and why? What is your opinion of this rule? Does this rule protect the attorney, the client, or both? If you were an attorney could you honor the rule at all required times?

Practice Test

True-False

_____1.   Practically speaking, today's adversary system is often more about negotiation than battle.

_____2.   Prosecutors can only obtain their office by way of public election.

_____3.   The chief law enforcement officer for a state or the United States is called "attorney general".

_____4.   Many observers opine that public defenders do not provide acceptable levels of defense.

_____5.   The grand jury determines guilt beyond a reasonable doubt.

_____6.   During arraignment, the facts of the case are reviewed to determine if probable cause to bind the defendant over for trial exists.

_____7.   "Information" is a charging instrument issued by the prosecutor.

_____8.   After a defendant enters a guilty plea, he or she is subsequently referred to the sentencing phase.

_____9.   Jail overcrowding may impact a judge's decision during bail setting.

_____10.   ROR is a condition of sentencing.

_____11.   Bail is provided for under the Sixth Amendment.

_____12.   As a result of *U.S. v. Salerno*, preventative detention was ruled to be unconstitutional.

_____13.   The Bail Reform Act of 1984 was criticized for failing to give judges the ability to detain persons that are deemed to be a danger to the immediate community.

_____14.   In the preliminary hearing, the magistrate decides if there is reasonable belief the defendant has committed the crime as charged.

_____15.   The grand jury consists of a group of citizens who have been impaneled to determine if probable cause exists to support (1) that a crime was committed and (2) that the suspect committed the crime.

_____16.   Defense counsel programs are designed to provide illiterate persons with a proper defense.

_____17.   *Nolo contendere* means "I will not contest the charge against me."

_____18.   The prosecutor is permitted to "overcharge" a defendant in order to induce a plea bargain.

_____19.   Prosecutors often evaluate a victim's credibility and reliability when screening cases for potential prosecution.

_____20.   *Strickland v. Washington* set the criteria for determining if one's legal representation was so poor as to deny Sixth Amendment rights.

Multiple Choice

1. Which one is NOT true about prosecutors?
    a. Prosecutors decide if arrested persons should be charged with crimes.
    b. Prosecutors decide if and when to stop prosecution.
    c. Prosecutors decide on the level or seriousness of the charges brought against a suspect.
    d. Prosecutors determine if a suspect is mentally competent to stand for trial.

2. The prosecutor is
    a. a passive member of the criminal justice process.
    b. a crime fighter who may or may not be a an elected official.
    c. essentially the same as a police chief.
    d. bound by attorney-client privilege.

3. Prosecutors are ultimately concerned with
    a. factual guilt.
    b. provable guilt.
    c. legal guilt.
    d. reasonable guilt.

4. The right to counsel is a protection provided under the
    a. Fourth Amendment.
    b. Fifth Amendment.
    c. Sixth Amendment.
    d. Eighth Amendment.

5. The modern role of the public defender was the result of the Supreme Court's ruling in
    a. *Gideon v. Wainwright*.
    b. *Miranda v. Arizona*.
    c. *Katz v. United States.*
    d. *Gates v. Collier*

6. Which one is NOT a part of the plea bargain process?
    a. Charge bargaining
    b. Sentence bargaining
    c. Count bargaining
    d. Cause bargaining

7. Release on Recognizance or ROR is
    a. facilitated by a bail bondsperson.
    b. ordered by a judge or other authorized judicial official.
    c. for first time offenders only.
    d. mandatory for all misdemeanor cases.

8. In discovery,

    a. the prosecutor seeks evidence for conviction from the defense.

    b. the judge sets the trial parameters for evidence.

    c. the defense seeks to obtain information from key case witnesses.

    d. the defense seeks to obtain case information from the prosecutor.

9. The grand jury

    a. must adhere to formal rules of law including the exclusionary rule.

    b. decides if the facts of the case rise to the level of probable cause.

    c. issues an "information".

    d. decides the issue of guilt or innocence.

10. *Nolle prosequi* occurs when

    a. a defendant pleads no contest.

    b. a defendant pleads not guilty.

    c. the prosecutor declines to prosecute a case.

    d. a defendant is found not guilty by way of bench trial.

11. Which would NOT be the subject matter of a pretrial motion?

    a. Change of venue

    b. Suppression of a procedure or action

    c. Request for case dismissal

    d. Request to poll the jury

12. The *Boykin* form

    a. is completed by a defendant who pleads "guilty."

    b. is completed by a defendant who pleads "no contest."

    c. is completed by a defendant who pleads "not guilty."

    d. is completed by indigent defendants who have been assigned counsel.

13. Which is NOT a defense attorney's responsibility or duty?

    a. Preparing the case for trial

    b. Supplying final approval for negotiated plea bargains

    c. Negotiating a sentence

    d. Investigating the criminal incident for which the defendant client has been charged

14. When local attorneys are asked to represent indigent defendants on a case-by-case basis, this is done as part of a(n)

    a. assigned counsel program.

    b. contracting attorney program.

    c. public defender program.

    d. mandatory counsel program.

15. According to the text, prosecutors and police may have some professional conflicts because
     a. police officers focus on factual guilt.
     b. prosecutors focus on legal guilt.
     c. they tend to come from different socio-economic backgrounds.
     d. of their political party affiliation.

16. One reason a defense attorney might desire a plea bargain is
     a. to wrap up the case as quickly as possible.
     b. to save time.
     c. because a review of the case facts reveals that the plea is in the client's best interest (best option on the table).
     d. it is the only way to assure conviction.

17. In the initial appearance phase of the justice process the accused person
     a. is sentenced.
     b. is asked to enter a plea on the charge(s).
     c. testifies.
     d. confronts witnesses.

18. Which one is NOT normally considered during the bail setting process?
     a. Uncertainty about a suspect's future behavior
     b. Risk
     c. Overcrowded jails
     d. The defendant's age

19. During the preliminary hearing,
     a. plea bargains receive their final approval.
     b. the suspect is asked to select (1) trial by jury or (2) trial by bench.
     c. evidence is presented.
     d. the suspect enters a plea to the charges.

20. Which of the following constitutes a true exception to the attorney-client privilege rule?
     a. If the client is mentally ill, privilege is waived.
     b. If the client discloses personal guilt in a capital offense, privilege is waived.
     c. If the client discloses the intent to commit a future crime, privilege is waived.
     d. If the client discloses a crime involving a sexual offense with a minor child victim, privilege is waived.

21. The prosecutor CANNOT
    a. choose how to prosecute a case.
    b. add charges to a case.
    c. dismiss the case or request the dismissal of charges.
    d. impose sentence on a defendant.

22. What does the prosecutor consider to be the most significant factor when evaluating a case for prosecution?
    a. Public sentiment about the case
    b. Police certainty of factual guilt
    c. Sufficiency of the known evidence
    d. Whether the victim will cooperate

23. Plea bargains negotiate every aspect of a case EXCEPT the
    a. primary charges.
    b. sentence.
    c. number of criminal counts.
    d. amount of good time to be credited to a defendant.

24. When a defendant pleads guilty in exchange for a reduction in charges, this is
    a. charge bargaining.
    b. sentence bargaining.
    c. count bargaining.
    d. offense bargaining.

25. What factor did the *Gideon v. Wainwright* case fail to issue guidance on?
    a. Whether or not a defendant is entitled to counsel
    b. A defendant's Sixth Amendment rights
    c. Exactly how indigent a defendant must be in order to receive public counsel
    d. Whether or not a defendant can have a fair trial without be afforded counsel

Fill in the Blank

1. Trial lawyers who initiate and conduct cases in the name of the people (government) are called _____.

2. The legal system where a court of law determines guilt or innocence based upon evidence that was presented by opposing parties is known as the_____system.

3. The lawyer responsible for representing the defendant is called the _____.

4. Court-appointed attorneys may be provided to _____ defendants.

5. Unless the defendant consents to disclosure, communication between client and attorney is subject to the _____ rule.

6. The defendant is advised of right to counsel, told of his or her bail, and given a date for the preliminary hearing during the _____ phase of the criminal justice process.

7. A grand jury issues a(n) _____ as a charging instrument.

8. Overcharging is a tactic used by _____ to induce a plea bargain from a criminal defendant.

9. A defendant who pleads _____ is in fact entering a "no contest" plea.

10. Salaried staff responsible for representing indigent defendants are generally part of a _____ program.

11. Preventive detention may be used if the case circumstances suggest the fear that the accused will commit additional _____ before trial.

12. Many courts now require a defendant to sign a _____ form as evidence that the defendant voluntarily waived all Constitutional rights that would attached at the time of trial.

13. The Supreme Court's ruling in _____ extends counsel and counsel related protections to juveniles.

Short Essays

1. List the different names given to public prosecutors and the general powers that they have.

2. Contrast the prosecutor's role as an elected official and as a crime fighter.

3. Delineate the responsibilities of defense attorneys.

4. Indicate the three types of defense allocation programs.

5. List the three basic features of an adversary system of justice.

6. Identify the steps involved in the pretrial criminal process.

7. Indicate the three influences on a judge's decision to set bail.

8. Explain how a prosecutor screens potential cases.

9. List and briefly explain the different forms of plea bargaining agreements.

10. Indicate the ways that both defense attorneys and prosecutors can induce plea bargaining.

Answer Key

True-False:
1. T, see pg. 318, LO5
2. T, see pg. 310, LO2
3. T, see pg. 309, LO1
4. T, see pg. 313, LO3
5. F, see pg. 326, LO6
6. F, see pg. 331, LO6
7. T, see pg. 326, LO6
8. T, see pg. 331, LO9
9. T, see pg. 322, LO7
10. F, see pg. 322, LO7
11. F, see pg. 321, LO7
12. F, see pg. 324, LO7
13. F, see pg. 324, LO7
14. F, see pg. 325, LO6
15. T, see pg. 326, LO6
16. F, see pg. 315, LO4
17. T, see pg. 331, LO9
18. T, see pg. 334, LO10
19. T, see pg. 330, LO8
20. T, see pg. 315, LO4

Multiple Choice:
1. d, see pg. 309, LO1
2. b, see pg. 310, LO2
3. c, see pg. 311, LO2
4. c, see pg. 312, LO3
5. a, see pg. 313, LO4
6. d, see pg. 332, LO9
7. b, see pg. 322, LO7
8. d, see pg. 326, LO6
9. b, see pg. 326, LO6
10. c, see pg. 329, LO8
11. c, see pg. 331, LO6
12. a, see pg. 335, LO10
13. b, see pg. 315, LO3
14. a, see pg. 315, LO4
15. d, see pg. 311, LO2
16. c, see pg. 333, LO9
17. a, see pg. 319, LO6
18. d, see pgs. 321-322, LO7
19. c, see pg. 325, LO6
20. c, see pg. 317, LO3
21. d, see pg. 309, LO1
22. c, see pgs. 329-330, LO8
23. d, see pg. 332, LO9
24. a, see pg. 332, LO9
25. c, see pg. 313, LO3

Fill in the Blank:
1. public prosecutor,
    see pg. 309, LO1
2. adversarial or adversary,
    see pg. 318, LO5
3. defense attorney,
    see pg. 313, LO3
4. indigent, see pg. 313, LO3
5. attorney-client privilege,
    see pg. 316, LO3
6. initial appearance,
    see pg. 319, LO6
7. indictment, see pg. 326, LO6
8. overcharging, see pg. 334, LO10
9. nolo contendere,
see pg. 331, LO6
10. public defender,
    see pg. 315, LO4
11. crimes, see pg. 324, LO7
12. Boykin, see pg. 335, LO10
13. *Gideon v. Wainwright*,
    see pg. 313, LO3

Short Essays:
1. See pgs. 309-311, LO1
2. See pg. 310, LO2
3. See pgs. 312-313, LO3
4. See pg. 313, LO4
5. See pg. 318, LO5
6. See pgs. 319-320, LO6
7. See pgs. 321-322, LO7
8. See pgs. 329-330, LO8
9. See pg. 332, LO9
10. See pg. 334, LO10

CHAPTER

10

THE CRIMINAL TRIAL

OUTLINE

- Special Features of Criminal Trials
- Jury Selection
- The Trial
- The Final Steps of the Trial and Postconviction Procedures
- Criminal Justice in Action—Rape Shield Laws

Learning Objectives

After reading this chapter, you should be able to:

LO1: Identify the basic protections enjoyed by criminal defendants in the United States

LO2: List the three requirements of the Speedy Trial Act of 1974.

LO3: Explain what "taking the Fifth" really means.

LO4: List the requirements normally imposed on potential jurors.

LO5: Contrast challenges for cause and peremptory challenges during *voir dire*.

LO6: List the standard steps in a criminal jury trial.

LO7: Explain the differences between testimony and real evidence; lay witnesses and expert witnesses; and direct and circumstantial evidence.

LO8: List possible affirmative defenses.

LO9: Delineate circumstances in which a criminal defendant may in fact be tried a second time for the same act.

LO10: List the six basic steps of an appeal.

Chapter Outline

I.   Special Features of Criminal Trials
  1. It is the state not the victim of the crime that brings the action against an alleged wrongdoer
  2. Trial procedures protect criminal defendants against the power of the state
  A. A "Speedy" Trial
    a. 6th Amendment
    b. Defendant loses right to move freely
    c. Potentially jeopardizes the persons reputation in the community
  2. Reasons for Delay
    a. Pretrial motions
    b. Plea negotiations
    c. Court congestion
  3. The Definition of a Speedy Trial
    i. When delay is unwarranted and proved to be prejudicial can accused claim a violation
    a. Speedy-trial laws
      i. Speedy Trial Act of 1974
        01. No more than 30 days between arrest and indictment
        02. No more than 10 days between indictment and arraignment
        03. No more than 60 days between arraignment and trial
    b. Statutes of limitations
      i. Legislative time limits that require prosecutors to charge a defendant with a crime

156

B. The Role of the Jury
    a. In all felony cases, defendant is entitled to jury trial
    b. Bench trial – judge decides questions of legality and fact
  1. Jury Size
    b. 12 person jury a historical accident
  2. Unanimity
    a. Jury verdicts must be unanimous for acquittal or conviction
C. The Privilege against Self-Incrimination
  1. 5th Amendment
D. The Presumption of Innocence
E. A Strict Standard of Proof
  1. Burden of proof lies with the state
  2. Beyond a reasonable doubt
  3. Social value – worse to convict an innocent person than let a guilty one go free

II. Jury Selection
A. Initial Steps: The Master Jury List and *Venire*
    a. Produce a cross section of the population
  1. Jury of Peers
    a. Ensures defendant is judged by members of the community
  2. The Master List
    a. Jury pool
    b. Jurors must be:
      i. Citizens
      ii. Over 18
      iii. No felony convictions
      iv. Healthy to serve in jury setting
      v. Sufficiently intelligent
  3. *Venire*
    a. List of people who are notified for jury duty
B. V*oir Dire*
    a. To speak the truth
    b. Written and oral questioning of potential jurors
  1. Challenging Potential Jurors
    a. Challenges for Cause
      i. Attorneys must provide a sound. legally justifiable reason
  2. Peremptory Challenges
    a. Attorney not required to give a reason
C. Race and Gender Issues in Jury Selection
    a. Instrument of de facto segregation
  1. The *Batson* Reversal
    a. Defendant must prove that the prosecution's use of a peremptory challenge was racially motivated
  2. Women on the Jury
    a. Extension of *Batson*
D. Alternate Jurors

157

III. The Trial
   A. Opening Statements
      1. Attorneys give brief version of the facts
   B. The Role of Evidence
      a. Evidence – anything used to prove the existence or nonexistence of a fact
      b. Testimony – statements by competent witnesses
      c. Real Evidence – includes physical items
      1. Testimonial Evidence
         a. Lay witness – average citizen
         b. Expert witness – scientific, medical, or technical skill
            i. May base opinions on:
               01. Facts or data of which they have personal knowledge
               02. Material presented at trial
               03. Secondhand information given to the expert outside the courtroom
      2. Direct versus Circumstantial Evidence
         a. Direct – witnessed by the person giving testimony
         b. Circumstantial – indirect evidence that establishes only the degree of likelihood of the fact
      3. Relevance
         a. Evidence that tends to prove or disprove a fact in question
      4. Prejudicial Evidence
         i. Evidence that tends to distract the jury from the main issue, mislead the jury, or cause an emotional response from jurors
         a. Real Evidence
         b. Evil Character
   C. The Prosecution's Case
      a. Presents corpus delicti of the crime to the jury
      1. Direct Examination of Witnesses
      2. Hearsay
         a. Any testimony given about a statement made by someone else
      3. Competence and Reliability of Witnesses
   D. Cross-Examination
      1. Questioning of an opposing witness during trial
      2. 6th Amendment's confrontation clause – accused shall enjoy the right to cross-examine witnesses
   E. Motion for a Directed Verdict
      1. Defense motion saying prosecution has not offered enough evidence to prove guilt
   F. The Defendant's Case
      1. Placing the Defendant on the Stand
      2. Creating a Reasonable Doubt
         a. Hung jury – reasonable doubt of just 1 juror
      3. Other Defense Strategies
         a. Alibi defense

    b. Affirmative defenses:
        i. Self-defense
        ii. Insanity
        iii. Duress
        iv. Entrapment
G. Rebuttal and Surrebuttal
    1. Rebuttal – prosecution bringing new evidence
    2. Surrebuttal – defense chance to cross-examine
H. Closing Arguments
    1. Attorneys summarize presentations
IV. The Final Steps of the Trial and Postconviction Procedures
A. Jury Instructions
    a. Charging the ury – judge sums up the case and instructs jurors on rules of law, during a charging conference
    1. The Judge's Role
    2. Understanding the Instructions
B. Jury Deliberation
    1. Majority Rules
    2. Restricting the Jury
    3. Sequestration
        a. Isolated from the public
C. The Verdict
    1. The Hung Jury
        a. Jury unable to agree unanimously
        b. *Allen* Charge – ask minority opinion jury members to consider majority opinion
    2. Jury Nullification
        a. Jurors nullify the law by acquitting a defendant according to the instructions given them by the court
D. Appeals
    1. Double Jeopardy
        i. Only available to defense
        b. The Limits of Double Jeopardy
        c. The Possibility and Risk of Retrial
    2. The Appeal Process
        a. Victim Appeals
            i. Crime Victims' Rights Act of 2004
E. Finality and Wrongful Convictions
    a. Finality – outcome of a criminal case can no longer be challenged by anyone
    1. Innocent after Being Proved Guilty
        a. The DNA Revolution: Part II
        b. Rethinking Finality
    2. Habeas Corpus
        a. You have the body
V. Criminal Justice in Action—Rape Shield Laws

159

Key Terms

Acquittal (pg. 347)
Allen Charge (pg. 368)
Appeal (pg. 369)
Bench trial (pg. 347)
Challenge for cause (pg. 353)
Charge (pg. 366)
Circumstantial evidence (pg. 358)
Closing arguments (pg. 365)
Confrontation clause (pg. 362)
Cross-examination (pg. 362)
Direct evidence (pg. 358)
Direct examination (pg. 360)
Double jeopardy (pg. 370)
Evidence (pg. 357)
Expert witness (pg. 357)
Finality (pg. 372)
Habeas corpus (pg. 374)
Hearsay (pg. 360)
Hung jury (pg. 368)
Jury nullification (pg. 369)
Jury trial (pg. 346)
Lay witness (pg. 357)
Master jury list (pg. 351)
Motion for a directed verdict (pg. 363)
Opening statements (pg. 356)
Peremptory challenges (pg. 354)
Real evidence (pg. 357)
Rebuttal (pg. 365)
Relevant evidence (pg. 359)
Statute of limitations (pg. 346)
Testimony (pg. 357)
Venire (pg. 351)
Verdict (pg. 368)
Voir dire (pg. 353)
Wrongful conviction (pg. 372)

Special Projects

1. Using popular media; research a criminal case that was successfully appealed (excluding DNA evidence based appeals). What was the basis for the appeal? What was the appellate court's decision?

2. Using popular media, research a criminal case where jury nullification occurred. Outline all of the circumstances surrounding this unusual event.

3. Take a close look at the *Bill of Rights*. Which of its Amendments do you feel is the most important and why?

Practice Test

True-False

_____1.   The Sixth Amendment provides for a speedy trial.

_____2.   A defendant is not required to have a jury trial.

_____3.   According to the U.S. Supreme Court, unanimity of a jury is not a rigid requirement for state trials but it is a requirement for federal trials.

_____4.   The high standard of proof required for conviction in a criminal trial reflects the social value that it is worse to convict an innocent person than to let a guilty person go free.

_____5.   A challenge for cause states the reason a prospective juror should be excused.

_____6.   In *Swain v. Alabama;* attorneys (prosecution and defense) were prohibited from striking jurors based upon race.

_____7.   Evidence is anything used to prove the existence or nonexistence of a fact.

_____8.   Evidence seen by, or described for, a jury in court is real evidence.

_____9.   Expert witnesses can testify about any evidence they are questioned about?

_____10.   Prospective jurors must be at least 21 years of age and free from felony convictions to be seated on a jury.

_____11.   For the most part, hearsay is admissible.

_____12.   A directed verdict is also known as a "motion for judgment as a matter of law" in the federal courts.

_____13.   An alibi is an affirmative defense.

_____14.   The "charge" sets forth the rules of law to be applied by the jury in deliberations.

_____15.   Double jeopardy is an absolute protection from multiple trials for the same offense.

_____16.   *Habeas corpus* is a court order directing that a defendant be brought before a federal court to hear claims concerning illegal detention.

Multiple Choice

1. Sixth Amendment rights include the
    a. right to be tried by an impartial jury.
    b. right to be free from cruel and unusual punishment.
    c. right to remain silent.
    d. right to be free from unreasonable search and seizure.

2. What party brings a criminal action against an alleged wrongdoer?
    a. Victim
    b. State
    c. Community
    d. Corporation

3. The Speedy Trial Act as amended in 1979 provides for all of the following EXCEPT
    a. no more than 60 days may lapse between arrest and indictment.
    b. no more than 30 days may lapse between indictment and arraignment.
    c. no more than 60 days may lapse between arraignment and trial.
    d. no more than 45 days may lapse between closing arguments and the verdict.

4. Which federal law provided procedural rights to victims?
    a. Speedy Trial Act of 1974
    b. Advocate Act of 1974
    c. Crime Victims Rights Act
    d. Procedural Due Process Act of 1981

162

5. The main goal of jury selection is
    a. to win the case.
    b. to have homogeneity.
    c. to produce a cross section of the population where the crime happened.
    d. to nullify the jury.

6. In most states jurors must
    a. be U.S. citizens.
    b. be registered with a recognized political party.
    c. be at least 21 years of age.
    d. have voted in the last presidential election.

7. *Voir dire* involves all of the following EXCEPT
    a. oral questioning of potential jurors.
    b. obtaining appropriate personal information from each juror.
    c. efforts to uncover juror biases.
    d. a criminal background query from the FBI

8. In *Batson v. Kentucky*, the United States Supreme Court ruled
    a. that defendants cannot try to prove that there has been discrimination during *venire*.
    b. that equal protection prohibits prosecutors from removing potential jurors on the basis of gender.
    c. that equal protection prohibits prosecutors from removing prospective jurors on the basis of race.
    d. that equal protection prohibits defense attorneys from removing prospective jurors on the basis of race.

9. In the opening statements the opposing attorneys
    a. attack the opponent's case.
    b. provide a road map for their presentation of evidence.
    c. introduce witnesses.
    d. begin presenting evidence.

10. Statements by competent witnesses, made under sworn oath, are called
    a. testimony.
    b. real evidence.
    c. direct evidence.
    d. circumstantial evidence.

11. Lay witnesses
   a. do not need to have specialized training in order to testify about a fact in question.
   b. need special training in order to testify about a fact in question.
   c. can stretch or exaggerate the facts (without penalty) in order to fit their personal or community view.
   d. cannot be prosecuted for perjury as they are not expected to be experts and have expert level knowledge about any matter.

12. Circumstantial evidence can be described by all of the following EXCEPT
   a. it is indirect evidence.
   b. it establishes likelihood of fact.
   c. it can create an inference that a fact exists.
   d. it must be physical in nature.

13. Prejudicial evidence
   a. is indirect and established through inference.
   b. is evidence that involves a racial or cultural bias.
   c. may distract from the main issues of the case.
   d. is consistent with the presumption-of-innocence standard.

14. The prosecutor attempts to establish guilt beyond a reasonable doubt by presenting the jury with the
   a. modus operandi.
   b. voir dire.
   c. corpus delecti.
   d. Habeus Corpus.

15. Hearsay evidence is generally not allowed for all of the following reasons EXCEPT
   a. the listener may have misunderstood.
   b. there can be no cross examination of the original statement maker.
   c. misconceptions cannot be challenged.
   d. it is usually ruled to be irrelevant gossip.

16. Which Amendment provides that a criminal defendant does not have to testify in his or her own defense?
   a. Fourth Amendment
   b. Sixth Amendment
   c. Fifth Amendment
   d. First Amendment

17. Possible affirmative defenses include
    a. alibi.
    b. mistaken identity.
    c. duress.
    d. casting a reasonable doubt.

18. California became the first state to require
    a. jury instructions in English.
    b. jury instructions in plain language.
    c. jury instructions in Braille.
    d. jury instructions displayed on large screens or large projections.

19. The appeals process is available to the
    a. prosecution and defense.
    b. defense only.
    c. prosecution only.
    d. victim's advocate.

20. In most states, which step would follow a defense closing statement?
    a. Prosecution's closing statement
    b. Motion for a directed verdict
    c. Prosecution rebuttal
    d. Defense surrebuttal

21. Jury nullification occurs when
    a. the jury cannot reach a verdict.
    b. the judge overrules the verdict submitted by the jury.
    c. the jury thinks the law is too lenient.
    d. the jury acquits in the face of irrefutable evidence of guilt.

22. Double jeopardy prohibits
    a. defendants from facing criminal and civil charges for the same offense.
    b. appeals after conviction.
    c. a defendant who has been acquitted from being tried again for the same offense in the same court.
    d. the defendant from being tried in federal and state courts for the same offense.

23. Finality in a criminal case relates to
    a. the end of a case, where it is no longer susceptible to challenge.
    b. the scientific standards for chemical and scientific evidence.
    c. the use of DNA test results on juvenile defendants.
    d. the assignment of the death penalty as punishment.

Fill in the Blank

1. A trial conducted without a jury is a _____ trial.

2. The right against self-incrimination is provided in the _____ Amendment.

3. In order to convict a person of a crime, guilt must be established beyond a _____.

4. The group of citizens from which the jury is selected is the _____.

5. A juror may be excused without a reason using a _____ challenge.

6. Verbal evidence given under oath by witnesses is _____.

7. Evidence that establishes the existence of a fact without relying on inference is _____.

8. Relevant evidence is evidence that tends to make a _____ in question more or less probable than it would be without the evidence.

9. The questioning of opposing witnesses during trial is _____.

10. The last arguments made after the cases have been presented are _____ arguments.

11. When the jury is isolated from the public, they are described as being _____.

12. The jury's formal decision in a case is the _____.

13. A jury whose members are irreconcilably divided in opinions is a _____.

14. In an *Allen* charge, the judge instructs jurors in a minority on a possible verdict to reconsider their _____.

15. When jurors acquit a defendant in spite of evidence of guilt, it is _____.

16. Seeking a higher court's review of a lower court's decision is a(n) _____.

17. The _____ Amendment provides an accused criminal defendant with the right to a speedy trial.

Short Essays

1. Identify the basic protections enjoyed by criminal defendants in the United States.

2. List the three requirements of the Speedy Trial Act of 1974.

3. Explain what "taking the Fifth" really means.

167

4. List the requirements normally imposed on potential jurors.

5. Contrast challenges for cause and peremptory challenges during *voir dire*.

6. List the standard steps in a criminal jury trial.

7. Explain the difference between testimony and real evidence; between lay witnesses and expert witnesses; and between direct and circumstantial evidence.

8. List possible affirmative defenses.

9. Delineate circumstances in which a criminal defendant may in fact be tried a second time for the same act.

10. List the six basic steps of an appeal.

Answer Key

True-False:
1. T, see pg. 345, LO1
2. T, see pg. 347, LO1
3. T, see pg. 347, LO1
4. T, see pg. 349, LO1
5. T, see pg. 353, LO5
6. F, see pg. 355, LO5
7. T, see pg. 357, LO7
8. F, see pg. 357, LO7
9. F, see pg. 357, LO7
10. F, see pg. 351, LO7
11. F, see pg. 360, LO7
12. T, see pg. 363, LO7
13. F, see pg. 364, LO8
14. T, see pg. 366, LO6
15. F, see pg. 370, LO9
16. T, see pg. 374, LO10

Multiple Choice:
1. a, see pg. 345, LO1
2. b, see pg. 345, LO1
3. d, see pg. 346, LO2
4. c, see pg. 340, LO10
5. c, see pg. 349, LO4
6. a, see pg. 351, LO4
7. d, see pg. 353, LO5
8. c, see pg. 354, LO5
9. b, see pg. 356, LO6
10. a, see pg. 357, LO7
11. a, see pg. 357, LO7
12. d, see pg. 358, LO7
13. c, see pg. 359, LO7
14. c, see pg. 360, LO7
15. d, see pg. 360, LO6
16. a, see pg. 347, LO1
17. c, see pg. 364, LO8
18. b, see pg. 364, LO6
19. b, see pg. 369, LO9
20. a, see pg. 365, LO6
21. d, see pg. 369, LO6
22. c, see pg. 370, LO9
23. a, see pg. 372, LO10

Fill in the Blank:
1. bench, see pg. 347, LO1
2. Fifth, see pg. 347, LO3
3. reasonable doubt,
      see pg. 348, LO1
4. *venire*, see pg. 351, LO4
5. peremptory, see pg. 354, LO5
6. testimony, see pg. 357, LO7
7. direct evidence,
      see pg. 358, LO7
8. fact, see pg. 359, LO7
9. cross examination,
      see pg. 362, LO6
10. closing, see pg. 365, LO6
11. sequestered, see pg. 368, LO6
12. verdict, see pg. 368, LO6
13. hung jury, see pg. 368, LO6
14. decision, see pg. 368, LO6
15. jury nullification,
      see pg. 369, LO6
16. appeal, see pg. 369, LO10
17. Sixth, see pg. 345, LO1

Short Essays:
1. See pgs. 345-349, LO1
2. See pg. 346, LO2
3. See pg. 347, LO3
4. See pg. 351, LO4
5. See pgs. 353-354, LO5
6. See pgs. 356-365, LO6
7. See pgs. 357-360, LO7
8. See pgs. 364-365, LO8
9. See pgs. 369-370, LO9
10. See pgs. 370-372, LO10

PUNISHMENT AND SENTENCING

OUTLINE

Learning Objectives

After reading this chapter, you should be able to:

LO1: List and contrast the four basic philosophical reasons for sentencing criminals.

LO2: Contrast indeterminate with determinate sentencing.

LO3: Explain why there is a difference between a sentence imposed by a judge and the actual sentence carried out by a prisoner.

LO4: List the six forms of punishment.

LO5: State who has input into the sentencing decision and list the factors that determine a sentence.

LO6: Explain some of the reasons why sentencing reform has occurred.

LO7: Identify the arguments for and against the use of victim impact statements during sentencing hearings.

LO8: Outline the Supreme Court rulings on capital punishment that led to the bifurcated process for death penalty sentencing.

LO9: Describe the main issues in the death penalty debate.

Chapter Outline

I. The Purpose of Sentencing
   A. Retribution
      1. Just Deserts
         a. Severity of the punishment must be in proportion to the severity of the crime
      2. Willful Wrongdoing
         a. Society is morally justified in punishing someone only if that person was aware that he or she committed a crime
   B. Deterrence
      a. Goal is to prevent future crimes
      1. General and Specific Deterrence
         a. General – Punishing one person will dissuade others
         b. Specific – an individual will be less likely to repeat act once punished
      2. Low Probability of Punishment
         a. For most crimes, wrongdoers are unlikely to be caught, sentenced, and imprisoned
   C. Incapacitation
      1. The Impact of Incapacitation
         a. Effective crime impact tool
      2. Selective and Collective Incapacitation
         a. Collective incapacitation – all offenders who have committed a similar crime are imprisoned for the same period of time

172

D. Rehabilitation
  1. Most humane goal of punishment
E. Restorative Justice
  1. Listening to the Victim
    a. Victims most interested in 3 things:
      i. Opportunity to participate in the process
      ii. Material reparation
      iii. Apology
  2. Limited Impact
II. The Structure of Sentencing
  A. Legislative Sentencing Authority
    1. Indeterminate Sentencing
      a. Set a minimum and maximum amount of time that a person must spend in prison
    2. Determinate Sentencing
      a. Fixed sentence
    3. Good Time and "Truth in Sentencing"
      a. Good time – a reduction in time served for good behavior
  B. Judicial Sentencing Authority
    1. Determinate encroachment on the power of judges
  C. Administrative Sentencing Authority
    1. Parole
    2. Parole Commissions
III. Individualized Justice and the Judge
  A. Forms of Punishment
    1. Capital Punishment
    2. Imprisonment
    3. Probation
    4. Fines
    5. Restitution and Community Service
    6. Apologies
  B. The Sentencing Process
    1. The Presentence Investigative Report
      a. Compiled by probation officer
      b. Describes:
        i. Crime in question
        ii. Suffering of any victim
        iii. Defendant's prior offenses
        iv. Defendant personal data
    2. The Prosecutor and the Defense Attorney
    3. Sentencing and the Jury
      a. Jury determines capital punishment
  C. Factors in Sentencing
    1. The Seriousness of the Crime
      a. Primary factor in judge's decision
      b. Real offense – actual behavior of the defendant

173

2. Mitigating and Aggravating Circumstances
    a. Mitigating – circumstances that allow for a lighter sentence
    b. Aggravating – circumstances that allow for harsher penalty
        i. Use of weapon
3. Judicial Philosophy

IV. Inconsistencies in Sentencing
  A. Sentencing Disparity
      a. Occurs when expectation of similar punishment for similar crime is not met in one of three ways:
          i. Criminals receive similar sentences for different crimes of unequal seriousness
          ii. Criminals receive different sentences for similar crimes
          iii. Mitigating or aggravating circumstances have a disproportionate effect on sentences
    1. Geographic Disparities
    2. Federal versus State Disparities
  B. Sentencing Discrimination
      a. Occurs when disparities can be attributed to extralegal variables such as the defendant's gender, race, or economic standing
    1. African Americans and Sentencing
        a. Comparing Sentences
        b. Crack Cocaine Sentencing
    2. Hispanics and Sentencing
    3. Women and Sentencing

V. Sentencing Reform
  A. Sentencing Guidelines
    1. State Sentencing Guidelines
        a. Minnesota first state - 1978
    2. Federal Sentencing Guidelines
        a. Sentencing Reform Act - 1984
    3. Judicial Departures
  B. Mandatory Sentencing Guidelines
      a. Limit a judge's power to deviate from determinate sentencing laws by setting firm standards for certain crimes
    1. Habitual Offender Laws
        a. Three strike laws
        b. "Three Strikes" in Court
            i. Upheld
        c. The consequences of "Three-Strikes" Laws
            i. Underused
  C. The Supreme Court and Determinate Sentencing
    1. A Return to Individualized Justice
  D. Victim Impact Evidence
      a. Victim impact statements – opportunity to testify during sentencing hearings about the suffering as a result of the crime
    2. Balancing the Process

3. The Risks of Victim Evidence
VI. Capital Punishment—The Ultimate Sentence
    a. Currently 3,300 convicts on death row
  A. The American Tradition of Capital Punishment
    1. Capital Punishment in the Seventeenth and Eighteenth Centuries
    2. Methods of Execution
  B. The Death Penalty and the Supreme Court
    1. *Weems v. United States*
      a. Cruel and unusual punishment is defined by the changing norms and standards of society and therefore is not based on historical interpretations
      b. Courts may decide whether a punishment is unnecessarily cruel with regard to physical pain
      c. Courts may decide whether a punishment is unnecessarily cruel with regard to psychological pain
    2. *Furman v. Georgia*
    3. The Bifurcated Process
    4. *Gregg v. Georgia*
    5. Mitigating Circumstances
      a. Insanity
      b. Mental Handicap
      c. Age
  C. Still Cruel and Unusual?
  D. Debating the Sentence of Death
    1. Deterrence
      a. For deterrence
      b. Against deterrence
    2. Incapacitation
    3. Fallibility
      i. Incapacitation Justification rests on 2 assumptions:
        01. Every convicted murderer is likely to recidivate
        02. The criminal justice system is infallible
    4. Arbitrariness
  E. Discriminatory Effect and the Death Penalty
    1. Race of the Victim
    2. Income of the victim
  F. The Immediate Future of the Death Penalty
    a. In decline since 1999
    1. Reasons for the Decline in Executions
    2. Continued Support for the Death Penalty
VII.   Criminal Justice in Action—The Morality of the Death Penalty

Key Terms

Aggravating circumstances (pg. 395)
Capital punishment (pg. 408)
Departure (pg. 402)
Determinate sentencing (pg. 389)
Deterrence (pg. 384)
"Good time" (pg. 389)
Habitual offender laws (pg. 402)
Incapacitation (pg. 385)
Indeterminate sentencing (pg. 388)
Just deserts (pg. 383)
Mandatory sentencing guidelines (pg. 402)
Mitigating circumstances (pg. 395)
Presentence investigative report (pg. 393)
"Real offense" (pg. 394)
Rehabilitation (pg. 386)
Restitution (pg. 387)
Restorative justice (pg. 386)
Retribution (pg. 383)
Sentencing discrimination (pg. 397)
Sentencing disparity (pg. 396)
Sentencing guidelines (pg. 400)
Truth-in-sentencing laws (pg. 389)
Victim impact statement (VIS) (pg. 405)

Special Projects

1. Research whether or not your state has the death penalty. Regardless of the answer ("yes" your state has the death penalty or "no" your state does not have the death penalty) identify a recent challenge to your state's law or its lack of legislation. What prompted the challenge? What was the outcome, if any?

2. Meet with a local area probation officer and conduct an interview with him or her about presentence investigation reports. What purpose do these reports serve? Who utilizes the finished reports? What is the scope of information in the report? What resources are used to compile the information in the report? Document your findings in a brief summary.

3. Research "three-strikes" type laws. Have these laws been adopted by the majority of states? Do you agree or disagree with them? Support your answer using your research.

Practice Test

True-False

_____1.   Retribution and revenge are the same thing.

_____2.   The willful principle of wrongdoing is central to the ideas of retribution.

_____3.   A fixed sentence that cannot be reduced by judges or administrative sentencing authorities is called a determinate sentence.

_____4.   Prisoners earn "good time" by following prison rules, and exhibiting overall good behavior.

_____5.   Truth-in-sentencing laws require inmates to serve 75% of their sentences.

_____6.   Parolees are inmates who are freed (released) from the legal custody and supervision of the state.

_____7.   Judges are not uniform or even consistent in their opinions concerning what is aggravating and what is mitigating.

_____8.   According to the Bureau of Justice Statistics, the average prison sentence handed out to African Americans and Caucasians in state courts was virtually the same.

_____9.   Judicial discretion in sentencing appears to be a double-edged sword; it allows judges to impose a wide variety of sentences but it also fails to reign in subjective personal bias.

_____10.   Judges are not allowed to depart from sentencing guidelines.

_____11.   Victim impact statements are statements made by a convicted offender to the victim or the victim's advocate.

_____12.   Cruel and unusual punishment is defined by the changing norms and standards of society and is not based on historical interpretation.

Multiple Choice

1. The oldest justification for punishment is
    a. retribution.
    b. deterrence.
    c. incapacitation.
    d. rehabilitation.

2. Incapacitation has several weaknesses that include all of the following EXCEPT
    a. a lack of proportionality.
    b. protection of society exists only during the incapacitation period.
    c. possible likelihood that offenders will commit more crime upon being freed.
    d. a low probability for punishment.

3. The most humane goal or philosophy of punishment is
    a. retribution.
    b. rehabilitation.
    c. deterrence.
    d. incapacitation.

4. Restitution is associated with
    a. rehabilitation.
    b. deterrence.
    c. restorative justice.
    d. retribution.

5. Which of the following is an administrative sentencing body?
    a. Parole board
    b. Judge
    c. Jury
    d. Legislature

6. Disillusionment with the ideals of rehabilitation led to the creation of
    a. parole.
    b. indeterminate sentencing.
    c. determinate sentencing.
    d. good time.

7. Aggravating circumstances include all of the following EXCEPT
    a. a prior criminal offense record.
    b. lack of judgment capacity.
    c. elements of duress.
    d. use of a weapon during the commission of a crime.

178

8. Mitigating circumstances include all of the following EXCEPT
    a. a prior criminal offense record.
    b. passive role in the offense.
    c. the age of the offender.
    d. elements of duress.

9. Which of the following may be signs of possible sentencing disparity?
    a. Different mitigating circumstances
    b. Different sentences for similar crimes
    c. Different aggravating circumstances
    d. Similar sentences for similar offenses

10. A sentencing disparity centering on the physical location where the offender was convicted is known as
    a. artificial disparity.
    b. sentencing discrimination.
    c. terrain disparity.
    d. geographic disparity.

11. According to the text, mandatory sentencing guidelines apply to all of the following crimes EXCEPT
    a. drug crimes.
    b. dangerous weapons crimes.
    c. habitual offender crimes.
    d. prostitution.

12. All of the following were the result of the Sentencing Reform Act EXCEPT
    a. elimination of parole for federal prisoners.
    b. limitations on early release.
    c. employment of a sentencing "grid" or matrix to guide decisions.
    d. sentences have been made more lenient overall.

13. Three-strikes laws raise constitutional concerns that this Amendment is being violated?
    a. Fourth Amendment
    b. Fifth Amendment
    c. Eighth Amendment
    d. Fourteenth Amendment

14. What criticisms have been made about victim impact statements (VIS)?
    a. Sentences should be based on emotion, not reason.
    b. The social value of the victim is brought into play rather than the circumstances of the crime.
    c. The social value of the offender is brought into play rather than the circumstances of the crime.
    d. The judge has access to too much information prior to sentencing.

15. The last public execution took place in Missouri in
   a. 1972.
   b. 1961.
   c. 1948.
   d. 1937.

16. In *Weems v. United States,* the Supreme Court ruled that
   a. what is cruel and unusual is defined by the changing norms of society.
   b. the death penalty is arbitrary.
   c. age is a mitigating circumstance when assigning the death penalty.
   d. that capital punishment is constitutional.

17. Roper v. Simmons prohibited the death penalty for
   a. insane persons.
   b. women.
   c. mentally challenged or handicapped persons.
   d. juveniles under age eighteen.

18. The death penalty argument includes debate over all of the following EXCEPT
   a. deterrence.
   b. arbitrariness.
   c. fallibility.
   d. individual vulnerability.

19. The number of executions has declined for all of the following reasons EXCEPT
   a. the outcome of the *Atkins* case.
   b. the outcome of the *Roper* case.
   c. new laws that provide for lifelong prison terms.
   d. the fact that crimes rates overall have been on a steady decline.

20. One of the primary arguments advocating the use of the death penalty, is that it prevents future crime because it satisfies
   a. the punishment goal of retribution.
   b. the punishment goal of deterrence.
   c. the punishment goal of rehabilitation.
   d. the punishment goal of just deserts.

Fill in the Blank

1. The principle that the severity of punishment should be determined by no other factor than the severity of the crime is _____.

2. The strategy of preventing crime through the threat of punishment is _____.

3. When criminals receive different sentences for the same offense, this is _____.

4. A strategy to prevent crime by detaining wrongdoers in prison is _____.

5. The philosophy that society is best served when wrongdoers are helped to eliminate crime from their behavior patterns is _____.

6. _____ statements are statements given to a sentencing authority by a victim as a means of telling the court about the personal impact of the crime.

7. The actual criminal behavior rather than the criminal _____ levied by the prosecutor is known as the real offense.

8. A document given to the judge, which assists with sentencing, and outlines the offender's life status and prior criminal history is known as a(n) _____ report.

9. *Roper v. Simmons* found that it was cruel and unusual to execute _____ offenders.

10. Determinate sentencing is essentially a _____ sentence.

Short Essays

1. List and contrast the four basic philosophical reasons for sentencing criminals.

2. Contrast indeterminate sentencing with determinate sentencing.

3. Explain why there is a difference between a sentence imposed by a judge and the actual sentence carried out by a prisoner.

4. List the six forms of punishment.

5. State who has input into the sentencing decision and list the factors that determine a sentence.

6. Explain some of the reasons why sentencing reform has occurred.

7. Identify the arguments for and against the use of victim impact statements during sentencing hearings.

8. Outline the Supreme Court rulings on capital punishment that led to the bifurcated process for death penalty sentencing.

9. Describe the main issues in the death penalty debate.

184

Answer Key

True-False:
1. F, see pg. 383, LO1
2. T, see pg. 383, LO1
3. T, see pg. 389, LO2
4. T, see pg. 389, LO3
5. F, see pg. 389, LO3
6. F, see pg. 390, LO3
7. T, see pg. 395, LO5
8. T, see pg. 398, LO6
9. T, see pg. 399, LO6
10. F, see pgs. 401-402, LO6
11. F, see pg. 405, LO7
12. T, see pg. 410, LO8

Multiple Choice:
1. a, see pg. 401, LO1
2. d, see pg. 385, LO1
3. b, see pg. 386, LO1
4. c, see pg. 387, LO1
5. a, see pg. 388, LO2
6. c, see pg. 389, LO2
7. c, see pg. 395, LO5
8. a, see pg. 395, LO5
9. b, see pg. 396, LO5/6
10. d, see pg. 397, LO5/6
11. d, see pg. 402, LO6
12. d, see pg. 400, LO6
13. c, see pg. 402, LO6
14. b, see pg. 407, LO7
15. d, see pg. 409, LO8
16. a, see pg. 410, LO8
17. d, see pg. 412, LO5/8
18. d, see pg. 418, LO9
19. d, see pg. 378, LO9
20. b, see pg. 413, LO9

Fill in the Blank:
1. just deserts, see pg. 383, LO1
2. deterrence, see pg. 384, LO1
3. sentencing disparity,
      see pg. 396, LO6
4. incapacitation, see pg. 385, LO1
5. rehabilitation, see pg. 386, LO1
6. victim impact, see pg. 405, LO7
7. charge, see pg. 394, LO5
8. presentence investigation,
      see pg. 393, LO5
9. juvenile, see pg. 412, LO9
10. fixed, see pg. 389, LO2

Short Essays:
1. See pgs. 383-388, LO1
2. See pg. 352, LO2
3. See pgs. 388-391, LO3
4. See pgs. 392-393, LO4
5. See pgs. 393-396, LO5
6. See pgs. 399-404, LO6
7. See pgs. 405-407, LO7
8. See pgs. 411-412, LO8
9. See pgs. 413-416, LO9

CHAPTER 12

PROBATION AND COMMUNITY CORRECTIONS

OUTLINE

- The Justification for Community Corrections
- Probation: Doing Time in the Community
- Intermediate Sanctions
- The Paradox of Community Corrections
- Criminal Justice in Action—California's Proposition 36

Learning Objectives

After reading this chapter, you should be able to:

LO1: Explain the justification for community-based corrections programs.

LO2: Indicate when probation started to fall out of favor, and explain why.

LO3: Explain several alternative sentencing arrangements that combine probation with incarceration.

LO4: Specify the conditions under which an offender is most likely to be denied probation.

LO5: Describe the three general categories of conditions placed on a probationer.

LO6: Explain why probation officers' work has become more dangerous.

LO7: Explain the three stages of probation revocation.

LO8: List the five sentencing options for a judge besides imprisonment and probation.

LO9: Contrast day reporting centers with intensive supervision probation.

LO10: List the three levels of home monitoring.

Chapter Outline

I.   The Justification for Community Corrections
     A. Reintegration
        1. Has a strong theoretical basis in rehabilitative theories of punishment
     B. Diversion
        1. Divert certain offenders away from prison and jail toward community correction alternatives
     C. The "Low-Cost Alternative"
II. Probation: Doing Time in the Community
        a. Most common form of punishment in the U.S.
        b. Probation – a criminal sanction in which a convict is allowed to remain in the community rather than be imprisoned as long as they follow certain conditions
     A. The Roots of Probation
        1. Judicial Reprieves – suspend sentences for a certain amount of time
        2. John Augustus and the Origins of Probation
           a. Boston shoemaker
        3. The Evolution of Probation
     B. Sentencing Choices and Probation
        1. Suspended Sentence
           a. Places no conditions or supervision on the offender
        2. Alternative Sentencing Arrangements
           a. Split Sentences

188

        i. Offender sentenced to a specific amount of time in prison or jail, to be followed by a period of probation
    b. Shock Incarceration
        i. Offender sentenced to prison or jail with understanding that probation may be granted
    c. Intermittent Incarceration
        i. Offender spends a certain amount of time each week in jail, workhouse, or other institution
C. Eligibility for Probation
    1. Individuals generally denied probation if:
        a. Convicted on multiple charges
        b. Was on probation or parole at time of arrest
        c. Have 2 or more prior convictions
        d. Are addicted to narcotics
        e. Seriously injured the victim
        f. Used a weapon
D. Conditions of Probation
        a. Contract between judge and offender
    1. Principles of Probation
    2. Types of Conditions
        a. Standard Conditions
            i.   Reporting to probation officer regularly
            ii. Notifying of any change of address
            iii. Not leaving the jurisdiction without permission
            iv. Remaining employed
        b. Punitive Conditions
            i.   Fines
            ii. Community service
            iii. Restitution
            iv. Drug testing
            v.   Home confinement
        c. Treatment Conditions
            i.   Drug or alcohol treatment
            ii. Anger-management treatment
E. The Supervisory Role of the Probation Officer
        a. Has two primary roles:
            i.   Conducting the presentence investigation
            ii. Supervisory
                01. Decentralized – under local, judicial control
                02. Centralized – under state, administrative control
    1. The Use of Authority
        a. Authority – ability to guide an offender successfully through the sentence
    2. The Offender's Perspective
    3. The Changing Environment of the Probation Officer
F. Revocation of Probation

189

      a. Probation ends in 1 of 2 ways:
         i. Completion of probation conditions
         ii. Revocation of probation
    1. Revocation Trends
      a. Technical violation – not a criminal violation but a break in the terms of probation
    2. The Revocation Process
      a. Preliminary Hearing
      b. Revocation Hearing
      c. Revocation Sentencing
G. Does Probation Work?
      a. Goal is to protect public safety
    1. The Hybrid Approach
      a. Mix of supervision and treatment seems to work best
    2. The Caseload Dilemma
      a. Caseload – number of clients a probation officer is responsible for at any one time
    3. New Models of Probation: Supervision with Treatment
         i. Outsourcing
      b. California's Proposition 36
         i. Mandates probation and community-based treatment for eligible drug offenders
      c. A Split Verdict
         i. Mixed results of proposition 36
III. Intermediate Sanctions
      a. Provides additional sentencing options
A. Judicially Administered Intermediate Sanctions
      a. Fines
      b. Community Service
      c. Restitution
      d. Forfeiture
      e. Pretrial Diversion Programs
    1. Forfeiture
      a. Government seizes property gained from or used in criminal activity
    2. Pretrial Diversion Programs
      a. During preliminary hearing
      b. Alternative to trial
    3. Drug Courts
      a. Fastest growing form of pretrial diversion in the country
B. Day Reporting Centers
      a. Mainly tools to reduce jail and prison overcrowding
C. Intensive Probation Supervision
    1. A more restrictive alternative to regular probation, with higher levels of face-to-face contact
D. Shock Incarceration

      a. Short period of incarceration that is designed to deter further criminal activity by shocking the offender with the hardships of imprisonment

    1. The Value of Shock

      a. Flash incarceration

    2. Boot Camps

      a. Offenders sent to a boot camp modeled on military basic training

E. Home Confinement and Electronic Monitoring

      a. Offenders serve sentences not in a government institution but at home

    1. The Levels of Home Monitoring and Their Benefits

      a. Curfew

      b. Home Detention

      c. Home Incarceration

    2. Types of Electronic Monitoring

      a. Programmed Contact

        i. Offender contacted periodically by telephone or beeper

      b. Continuous Signaling

        i. Worn around wrist, ankle, or neck

    3. Technological Advances in Home Confinement

    4. Effectiveness of Home Confinement

F. Widening the Net

    1. Criticism that intermediate sanction designed to divert offenders from prison actually increase the number of citizens who are under the control of the corrections system

IV. The Paradox of Community Corrections

      a. The more effectively offenders are controlled, the more likely they are caught violating the terms of their conditional release

A. "Quicksand Effect"

    1. Pulls offenders more deeply into the correctional system

V. Criminal Justice in Action—California's Proposition 36

Key Terms

Authority (pg. 436)

Caseload (pg. 440)

Day reporting centers (pg. 445)

Diversion (pg. 430)

Electronic monitoring (pg. 447)

Forfeiture (pg. 443)

Home confinement (pg. 447)

Intensive supervision probation (ISP) (pg. 446)

Intermediate sanctions (pg. 442)

Judicial reprieve (pg. 431)

Pretrial diversion program (pg. 443)

Probation (pg. 431)
Reintegration (pg. 429)
Shock incarceration (pg. 446)
Split sentence probation (pg. 431)
Suspended sentence (pg. 431)
Technical violation (pg. 437)
Widen the net (pg. 450)

Special Projects

1. Interview a probation officer and find out what community based sanctions are used in offender sentencing. Are there any that the text did not include?

2. Attend a local court sentencing proceeding. What community based sanctions were administered? What was the most common form of sanction? How many cases involved some form of community based sanction?

3. Research global positioning systems (GPS) as electronic monitoring devices for sentenced offenders. Identify the costs associated with administering these programs. What cost does the offender pay, if any? Are they cost prohibitive or a value?

Practice Test
True-False

_____1.   More than four million adults are on probation in the U.S.

_____2.   Intensive probation, fines, boot camps, and electronic monitoring are all forms of community based sanctions.

_____3.   The father of probation is Robert Peel.

_____4.   The judge may jail an offender for violation of conditions of a suspended sentence.

_____5.   Offenders who are addicted to narcotics are unlikely to be assigned probation.

_____6.   The ideal probation officer-client relationship is based on the clients respect for authority.

_____7.   Some probationers see supervised probation as akin to "baby sitting."

_____ 8. Curfew is a form (or level) of home monitoring.

_____ 9. Probation revocation is a two-step process; the first step involves a probation violation and the second step involves a revocation hearing.

_____ 10. Those who cannot afford to pay for electronic monitoring may not be eligible for it.

Multiple Choice

1. Approximately how many adults are under the supervision of state and federal probation agencies?
     a. 1 million
     b. 4 million
     c. 2 million
     d. 8 million

2. In general, what type of punishment does public popular opinion favor over community based corrections?
     a. Rehabilitation
     b. Reintegration
     c. Retribution
     d. Treatment

3. Which of the following best describes the sanction where an offender spends a certain amount of time each week incarcerated but is free in the community the remainder of the time?
     a. Split sentence
     b. Shock incarceration
     c. Intermittent incarceration
     d. Suspended sentence

4. When offenders spend a specific amount of time in jail, followed by a period of probation, they were sentenced to
     a. a split sentence.
     b. shock incarceration.
     c. intermittent incarceration.
     d. a suspended sentence.

5. Offenders are more likely to be denied probation if they
    a. are convicted of multiple charges.
    b. show a lack of remorse.
    c. are addicted to alcohol.
    d. are illiterate.

6. The principles of probation operate under all of the following principles EXCEPT
    a. to serve to rehabilitate the offender.
    b. to protect the community.
    c. to be constitutional.
    d. to be free from religious influence.

7. The *standard conditions* of probation involve
    a. regular reporting to a probation officer.
    b. attending church on a regular basis.
    c. treatment options.
    d. community service.

8. Contemporary probation officers perform all of the following functions EXCEPT
    a. surveillance operations.
    b. search and seizure operations.
    c. the administration of substance (drug) testing.
    d. presiding over a revocation hearing.

9. In *Mempa v. Rhay*, the court ruled that
    a. probation cannot be revoked for a technical violation.
    b. probationers have the right to counsel during revocation hearings.
    c. probation officers may not revoke probation without a hearing.
    d. probationers are entitled to a jury during revocation proceedings.

10. The first stage of the probation revocation procedure is the
    a. revocation hearing.
    b. revocation sentencing.
    c. preliminary hearing.
    d. arraignment.

11. Parole revocation is generally a
    a. two-step process.
    b. five-step process.
    c. one-step process.
    d. three-step process

12. When it comes to the probation officer/client relationship, in the absence of trust, probation officers must rely on
    a. authority.
    b. force.
    c. manipulation.
    d. threats.

13. Intermediate sanctions do not include
    a. fines.
    b. restitution.
    c. parole.
    d. forfeiture.

14. Which of the following is an example of shock incarceration?
    a. Day treatment
    b. Boot camp
    c. Drug court
    d. Electronic monitoring

15. The most restrictive level of home monitoring is
    a. curfew.
    b. home detention.
    c. home incarceration.
    d. electronic monitoring.

16. The benefits of home confinement include all of the following EXCEPT
    a. community protection.
    b. saving facility space.
    c. the idea that it meets public expectation for punishment.
    d. the seizure of assets under forfeiture.

17. All of the following are types of probation conditions EXCEPT
    a. punitive conditions.
    b. standard conditions.
    c. treatment conditions.
    d. forfeiture conditions.

18. An offender can enter a drug court program
    a. after arrest or at conviction.
    b. while on parole.
    c. while on probation for a first offense.
    d. if the offender is under the age of 21 and has no prior criminal history.

19. Punitive probation conditions include all of the following EXCEPT
    a. fines.
    b. drug testing.
    c. regular reporting to probation officer.
    d. community service.

20. The fastest growing form of pretrial diversion in the country is
    a. electronic monitoring.
    b. drug court.
    c. anger management programming.
    d. domestic violence counseling.

21. Forfeiture allows the seizure of property gained from illegal activity under the
    a. Holmes-Smithfield Act.
    b. Sentencing Reform Act.
    c. Can-SPAM Act.
    d. 1970 RICO Act.

22. The father of probation is
    a. Robert Peel.
    b. August Vollmer.
    c. John Augustus.
    d. John Clockars.

23. Probationers in the United States account for
    a. nearly two-thirds of all adults in the corrections population.
    b. nearly three-quarters of all of the adults in the corrections population.
    c. nearly one-third of all adults in the corrections population.
    d. nearly one-half of all adults in the corrections population.

24. Probation accounts for
    a. nearly two thirds of the corrections population.
    b. about twenty percent of the adult citizens of the nation.
    c. the most serious convicts.
    d. only first-time offenders.

25. Reintegration means all of the following EXCEPT
    a. restoring family ties.
    b. facilitating employment.
    c. securing a place for the offender in society.
    d. just deserts.

Fill in the Blank

1. A corrections goal that focuses on returning the offender to the community is _____.

2. The strategy to move qualified offenders away from institutional corrections and toward community-based and intermediate sanctions is _____.

3. Reintegration has a strong theoretical basis in the _____ philosophy of punishment.

4. An offender who is identified as being _____ to narcotics is generally not eligible for probation.

5. Postponement of sentence on the order of the judge is _____.

6. Split sentence probation is also known as _____.

7. The ideal probation officer–offender relationship is based on _____.

8. Weekly meetings with a probation officer is considered a _____ condition of probation.

9. Home confinement can involve _____ monitoring.

10. The wisdom of the street has it that the inspiration for electronic monitoring came from a _____ comic book.

Short Essays

1. Explain the justification for community-based corrections programs.

2. Indicate when probation started to fall out of favor, and explain why.

3. Explain several different kinds of sentencing arrangements that combine probation with incarceration.

4. Specify the conditions under which an offender is most likely to be denied probation.

198

5. Describe the three general categories of conditions placed on a probationer.

6. Explain why probation officers' work has become more dangerous.

7. Explain the three stages of probation revocation.

8. List the five sentencing options for a judge besides imprisonment and probation.

9. Contrast day reporting centers with intensive supervision probation.

10. List the three levels of home monitoring.

Answer Key

True-False:
1. T, see pg. 428, LO1
2. T, see pg. 429, LO1
3. F, see pg. 432, LO2
4. T, see pg. 433, LO3
5. T, see pgs. 433-434, LO4
6. F, see pg. 436, LO6
7. T, see pg. 437, LO6
8. T, see pg. 447, LO10
9. F, see pg. 439, LO7
10. T, see pg. 450, LO10

Multiple Choice:
1. b, see pgs. 430-431, LO1
2. c, see pg. 429, LO1
3. c, see pg. 433, LO3
4. a, see pg. 433, LO3
5. a, see pg. 434, LO4
6. d, see pg. 434, LO5
7. a, see pg. 435, LO5
8. d, see pg. 437, LO6
9. b, see pg. 439, LO7
10. c, see pg. 439, LO7
11. d, see pg. 439, LO7
12. a, see pg. 436, LO6
13. c, see pg. 442, LO8
14. b, see pg. 447, LO8
15. c, see pg. 448, LO10
16. d, see pg. 448, LO10
17. d, see pg. 435, LO5
18. a, see pg. 444, LO8
19. c, see pg. 435, LO5
20. b, see pg. 444, LO8
21. d, see pg. 443, LO8
22. c, see pg. 432, LO1/2
23. a, see pg. 431, LO1
24. a, see pg. 430, LO1
25. d, see pg. 429, LO1

Fill in the Blank:
1. reintegration, see pg. 429, LO1
2. diversion, see pg. 430, LO1
3. rehabilitation, see pg. 429, LO1
4. John Augustus,
   see pg. 432, LO2
5. addicted, see pg. 434, LO4
6. shock probation,
   see pg. 433, LO3
7. trust, see pg. 436, LO6
8. standard, see pg. 435, LO5
9. electronic, see pg. 447, LO10
10. Spiderman, see pg.448, LO10

Short Essays:
1. See pgs. 429-430, LO1
2. See pgs. 431-432, LO2
3. See pg. 433, LO3
4. See pgs. 433-434, LO4
5. See pgs. 434-435, LO5
6. See pg. 437, LO6
7. See pg. 439, LO7
8. See pg. 442, LO8
9. See pgs. 445-447, LO9
10. See pgs. 447-449, LO10

PRISONS AND JAILS

OUTLINE

Learning Objectives

After reading this chapter, you should be able to:

LO1: Contrast the Pennsylvania and the New York penitentiary theories of the 1800s.

LO2: List the factors that have caused the prison population to grow dramatically in the last several decades.

LO3: Explain the three general models of prisons.

LO4: List and briefly explain the four types of prisons.

LO5: Describe the formal prison management system, and indicate the three most important aspects of prison governance.

LO6: List the reasons why private prisons can often be run more cheaply than public ones.

LO7: Summarize the distinction between jails and prisons, and indicate the importance of jails in the American correctional system.

LO8: Explain how jails are administered.

LO9: Indicate the difference between traditional jail design and new-generation jail design.

LO10: Indicate some of the consequences of our high rates of incarceration.

Chapter Outline

I. A Short History of American Prisons
    A. Walnut Street Prison: The First Penitentiary
        a. Penitentiary – an early form of correctional facility that emphasized separating inmates from society and from each other
        b. Eventually succumbed to overcrowding and excessive cost
    B. The Great Penitentiary Rivalry: Pennsylvania versus New York
        1. The Pennsylvania System
        a. Separate Confinement
            i. Inmates kept separate from each other at all times, daily activities took place in separate cells
        2. The New York System
        a. Congregate System
            i. Also known as the Auburn system
            ii. Inmates kept in separate cells during the night, but worked together in the day
    C. The Reformers and the Progressives
        1. The "New Penology"
        2. Elmira
        3. The Medical Model
        a. Institutions should offer a variety of programs and therapies to cure inmates of their ills
    D. The Reassertion of Punishment

II. The Prison Population Bomb
- a. Population of prisons or jails have more than tripled since 1985

A. Factors in Prison Population Growth
- a. Consequence of penal harm movement, get tough ideologies
  - i. Enhancement of Drug Laws
  - ii. Increased Probability of Incarceration
- b. Federal Prison Growth
- c. Rising Incarceration Rates of Women

B. The Prison Construction Boom

III. The Role of Prisons in Society

A. Different schools of thought behind prison organization
1. Custodial Model
   - a. Prisons are incarcerated for reasons of incapacitation, deterrence, and retribution
2. Rehabilitation Model
   - a. Stresses the ideals of individualized treatment
3. Reintegration Model
   - a. Serves as training ground for the inmate to prepare for existence in the community

IV. Types of Prisons
1. Federal prison inmate security levels
   - a. 1 is lowest amount of security, 6 is harshest security measures

A. Maximum Security Prisons
- a. Houses offenders with extensive records, violent, and repeated offenders
1. The Design
   - a. Tend to be large, holding more than 1000 inmates
2. Supermax Prisons
   - i. Reserved for the worst of the worst of America's corrections populations
   - a. A Controlled Environment
     - i. Operate in a state of perpetual lockdown, all inmates are confined to their cells and social activities nonexistent
   - b. Supermax Syndrome
     - i. Inmates manifest a number of psychological problems, including massive anxiety, hallucinations, and acute confusion

B. Medium and Minimum Security Prisons
1. Medium security prisons – inmates have committed less serious crimes and not considered high risks for escaping or causing harm
2. Minimum security prisons – inmates are first time offenders who are nonviolent and well behaved, high percentage are white-collar

V. Prison Administration

A. Formal Prison Management
1. Chain of command
2. Continuity of Purpose
3. Warden ultimately responsible for the operation of a prison

B. Governing Prisons
  1. Order
  2. Amenities
  3. Services
VI. The Emergence of Private Prisons
  A. Why Privatize?
    1. Cost Efficiency
      a. Labor costs
      b. Competitive building
      c. Less red tape
    2. Overcrowding and Outsourcing
    3. Quality of Service
  B. The Argument Against Private Prisons
    1. Safety Concerns
    2. Financial Concerns
    3. Philosophical Concerns
  C. The Future of Privatization in the Corrections Industry
    1. Industry assured by 2 factors:
      a. Shrinking budgets force states to look for alternatives
      b. BOP has turned to private prisons to expand capacity
VII. Jails
  A. The Function of Jails
    1. Hold convicted misdemeanors
    2. Receive individuals pending arraignment
    3. Temporarily hold juveniles
    4. Hold mentally ill pending transfer to health facilities
    5. Detain those who have violated conditions of probation
    6. House inmates awaiting transfer to federal or state prisons
    7. Operate community-based corrections
  B. The Jail Population
    1. Pretrial Detainees
      a. Have been arrested by police and are unable to post bail
    2. Sentenced Jail Inmates
      a. Time served – judge often will credit the length of time the convict has spent in detention waiting trial
      b. Acknowledges 2 realities of jails
        i. Terms are generally too short to allow the prisoner to gain any benefit
        ii. Jails are chronically overcrowded
    3. Other Jail Inmates
      a. Pretrial detainees and those convicted of misdemeanors make up the majority of the jail population
  C. Jail Administration
      a. 3,370 jails in the U.S., 2,700 operated on a county level by an elected sheriff
    1. The "Burden" of Jail Administration

206

Key Terms

Special Projects

1. Research the infamous "Alcatraz" prison and prepare a report on its history. Identify some of the myths associated with it. Why does it continue to be a top tourist destination? Identify several of the more famous inmates.

2. Do some job hunting; research warden's positions and locate the related job description. Summarize what you learned in a short report and identify (1) the

professional experience requirements, (2) educational requirements, (3) general duties and responsibilities, and (4) salary and benefits package.

3. Read up on "supermax prisons." What did you learn as a result of your reading? Are these structures the most secure? Are there any plans to build more? How many supermax prisons are in operation in the U.S. today?

Practice Test

True-False

_____1. Rehabilitation is included as one of the goals of the custodial model.

_____2. The American colonies differed very little from England's punishment philosophy.

_____3. About 87 percent of the jail population is male.

_____4. The Walnut Street prison was a failure.

_____5. The New York system of confinement is also known as the Auburn system.

_____6. Robert Martinson eventually retracted most of the claims he made in "What Works?"

_____7. Some criminologists think that imprisonment and lengthy prison terms are directly responsible for dropping crime rates.

_____8. The majority of prison inmates are held in maximum security facilities.

_____9. Private prisons can be run more cost efficiently than state penitentiaries.

_____10. The traditional jail utilizes a podular design.

Multiple Choice

1. Incarceration rates have increased dramatically, primarily due to
    a. terrorism.
    b. harsher penalties for sex offenders.
    c. the war on drugs.
    d. the increasing number of juveniles tried and incarcerated as adults.

2. The number of women incarcerated today has
   a. remained stable.
   b. slowly decreased.
   c. slowly increased.
   d. rapidly increased.

3. Which prison organization model stresses individualized treatment?
   a. Custodial model
   b. Rehabilitation model
   c. Retribution model
   d. Reintegration model

4. In Federal prisons, inmates are lodged by categorizing them into
   a. three security levels.
   b. four security levels.
   c. six security levels.
   d. eight security levels.

5. Within a typical correctional facility, who is responsible for the overall performance and operation of the correctional facility?
   a. Assistant warden
   b. Corrections officers
   c. Warden
   d. Governor

6. Private prisons can be run more cost effectively run than public prisons. Of the following which is NOT a reason for this?
   a. Private prisons have lower labor costs.
   b. Private prisons do not have to provide inmate programs and services.
   c. Private prisons can access private markets to obtain competitive bids.
   d. Private prisons have less managerial red tape.

7. The main difference between police agencies and correctional facilities is that correctional facilities lack
   a. a chain of command.
   b. bureaucracy.
   c. continuity of purpose.
   d. a military structure.

8. Arguments against private prisons include
   a. there is too much red tape involved in their management.
   b. cutting corners by the operators.
   c. conditions are primitive and unsanitary.
   d. they are too expensive.

9. Jails do not
   a. hold misdemeanants.
   b. receive individuals pending arraignment.
   c. serve as a primary place for the mentally ill to be treated.
   d. operate community based corrections programs.

10. When a judge gives an offender credit for days spent in jail awaiting trial, this is called
   a. good time.
   b. time served.
   c. probation.
   d. a suspended sentence.

11. Jail designs include all of the following EXCEPT
   a. podular.
   b. traditional.
   c. linear design.
   d. campus style.

12. In direct supervision jails,
   a. the pods are isolated from the staff.
   b. communication between inmates and staff is impeded by infrastructure.
   c. there is usually a lower comfort level for inmates than in traditional jails.
   d. officers are able to address misconduct more quickly and efficiently.

13. Disenfranchisement refers to
   a. barring convicts from obtaining driver's licenses.
   b. taking away convict's ability to participate in mainstream society.
   c. taking away a convict's right to a democratic vote.
   d. violating the civil right of inmates.

14. Of the following, which crime could subject a convicted offender to placement into a supermax facility?
   a. Murder of a fellow inmate
   b. Unarmed robbery
   c. Sex crimes against children
   d. Embezzlement

15. Supermax prisons keep inmates in a state of lockdown, which means
   a. inmates are kept in their cells 22 ½ hours each day, and released only to shower or exercise.
   b. inmates are kept in total isolation.
   c. inmates may eat together, but are kept in shackles.
   d. inmates are kept in their cells 24 hours a day.

16. The anxiety, hallucinations, and confusion experienced by supermax inmates has been described as
    a. temporary insanity.
    b. schizophrenia.
    c. supermax syndrome.
    d. acute psychosis.

17. The function of 18th Century incarceration facilities in England involved all of the following EXCEPT
    a. holding debtors.
    b. holding those to be exiled.
    c. holding those to be executed.
    d. holding vagrants.

18. Which one is NOT associated with the American colonies correctional system?
    a. It differed little from England's system
    b. It used more corporal punishment than England
    c. It held debtors
    d. It was constructed of a podular design

19. The "new penology"
    a. awarded early release opportunities.
    b. involved total segregation for inmates.
    c. kept inmates in total silence.
    d. assigned inmates to work at hard labor.

20. The Progressives believed that
    a. prisons should offer a variety of programs to "cure" inmates.
    b. prisons should provide inmates with time to pray and repent.
    c. prisons should be designed to punish inmates.
    d. prisons should train inmates to work in the outside world.

21. Folsom, Attica, and Sing Sing are all examples of
    a. medium security prison facilities.
    b. maximum security prison facilities.
    c. supermax prison facilities.
    d. federal prison facilities.

22. With regard to high incarceration rates, compared to twenty years ago, federal inmates are
    a. serving about 50% less time.
    b. serving about the same amount of time.
    c. serving about 50% more time.
    d. being directed back into the community at a greater rate.

23. Which concept is NOT associated with the reintegration model?
    a. Prisoners progressive responsibility
    b. Providing work opportunities
    c. Preparing inmates for release
    d. Stressing incarceration over return to society

24. With regard to the custodial model,
    a. all decisions in prison are made with security as a primary focus.
    b. inmates are provided opportunities for work.
    c. inmates are prepared for release into society.
    d. it assumes that prisoners are incarcerated for rehabilitation.

25. Which of the following designs best describes a prison that makes prisoner observation easier by way of a long central corridor?
    a. Radial design
    b. Campus style
    c. Courtyard style
    d. Telephone-pole design

Fill in the Blank

1. The first great swing in American incarceration policy was brought about by the _____.

2. A correctional facility that emphasizes reflecting on one's wrongdoing and pondering one's reformation is a _____.

3. Separate confinement was the primary concept of the _____ system.

4. The New York system emphasizes a method of living called the _____ system.

5. A prison facility usually constructed of cement walls and electronic barriers to hold dangerous offenders is best described as a _____ level prison.

6. A prison that is designed to hold the "worst of the worst" offender(s) is a _____ level prison.

7. A correctional institution designed to allow inmates a great deal of freedom and contact with the outside world is a _____ level prison.

8. A _____ is a county facility used to hold offenders awaiting trial as well as sentenced misdemeanor offenders.

9. New-generation jails are constructed in a _____ design.

10. Inmates who are held in jail prior to adjudication (including conviction) are known as _____ detainees.

Short Essays

1. Contrast the Pennsylvania and the New York penitentiary theories of the 1800s.

2. List the factors that have caused the prison population to grow dramatically in the last several years.

3. Explain the three general models of prisons.

4. List and briefly explain the four types of prisons.

5. Describe the formal prison management system and the three most important aspects of prison governance.

6. List the reasons why private prisons can be run more cheaply than public ones in the American correctional system.

7. Summarize the distinction between jails and prisons, and indicate the importance of jails in the American correctional system.

8. Explain how jails are administered.

9. Indicate the difference between traditional jail design and new-generation jail design.

10. Indicate some of the consequences of our high rate of incarceration.

Answer Key

True-False:
1. F, see pg. 468, LO3
2. T, see pg. 461, LO1
3. T, see pg. 482, LO7
4. T, see pg. 462, LO1
5. T, see pg. 462, LO1
6. T, see pg. 464, LO1
7. T, see pg. 464, LO2
8. F, see pg. 473, LO4
9. T, see pg. 477, LO6
10. F, see pg. 486, LO9

Multiple Choice:
1. c, see pg. 465, LO2
2. d, see pg. 466, LO2
3. b, see pg. 468, LO3
4. c, see pg. 468, LO4
5. c, see pg. 474, LO5
6. b, see pg. 477, LO6
7. c, see pg. 474, LO5
8. b, see pg. 478, LO6
9. c, see pg. 481, LO8
10. b, see pg. 483, LO8
11. d, see pgs. 485-486, LO8
12. d, see pgs. 485-486, LO9
13. c, see pg. 488, LO10
14. a, see pg. 471, LO4
15. a, see pg. 472, LO4
16. c, see pg. 472, LO4
17. d, see pg. 461, LO1
18. d, see pg. 461, LO1
19. a, see pg. 463, LO1
20. a, see pg. 463, LO1
21. b, see pg. 469, LO4
22. c, see pg. 466, LO2
23. d, see pg. 468, LO3
24. a, see pg. 468, LO3
25. d, see pg. 470, LO3

Fill in the Blank:
1. Quakers, see pg. 461, LO1
2. penitentiary, see pg. 461, LO1
3. Pennsylvania, see pg. 462, LO1
4. Congregate, see pg. 462, LO1
5. maximum security,
    see pg. 469, LO4
6. supermax, see pg. 471, LO4
7. minimum security,
    see pg. 473, LO4
8. jail, see pg. 480, LO8
9. podular, see pg. 486, LO8
10. pretrial, see pg. 482, LO8

Short Essays:
1. See pgs. 462-464, LO1
2. See pgs. 464-466, LO2
3. See pgs. 467-468, LO3
4. See pgs. 468-474, LO4
5. See pgs. 474-475, LO5
6. See pgs. 477-480, LO6
7. See pgs. 480-483, LO7
8. See pgs. 483-485, LO8
9. See pgs. 485-486, LO9
10. See pg. 487, LO10

BEHIND BARS

The Life of an Inmate

OUTLINE

- Prison Culture
- Prison Violence
- Inside a Women's Prison
- Correctional Officers and Discipline
- Protecting Prisoners' Rights
- Parole and Release from Prison
- Reentry into Society
- Criminal Justice in Action—A Second Look at Residency Laws

Learning Objectives

After reading this chapter, you should be able to:

LO1:   Explain the concept of prison as a total institution.

LO2:   Describe the possible patterns of inmate behavior, which are driven by the inmate's personality and values.

LO3:   Indicate some of the reasons for violent behavior in prisons.

LO4:   List and briefly explain the six general job categories among correctional officers.

LO5:   Contrast the hands-off doctrine of prisoner law with the hands-on approach.

LO6:   Contrast probation, parole, mandatory release, pardon and furlough.

LO7:   Describe truth-in-sentencing laws and their goals.

LO8:   Describe typical conditions of parole.

LO9:   Explain the goal of prisoner reentry programs.

LO10: Indicate typical conditions for release of a paroled child molester.

Chapter Outline
I. Prison Culture
   A. The Total Institution
         a. Encompass every aspect of an inmate's life
   B. Who Is in Prison
         a. Rates of minorities and women have increased sharply
      1. The Aging Inmate Population
      2. An Ailing Inmate Population
   C. Adapting to Prison Society
      1. Prisonization
         a. Adapting to the prison culture
II. Prison Violence
   A. Violence in Prison Culture
      1. Violence:
         a. Provides deterrence against being victimized
         b. Enhances self-image
         c. Gives sexual relief in case of rape
         d. Serves as a means of acquiring material goods
      2. Deprivation Model
         a. Stressful and oppressive conditions lead to aggressive behavior
   B. Riots
         a. Loss of Institutional Control
         b. Relative Deprivation
      1. The Spectrum of Violence
         a. Attica
   C. Issues of Race and Ethnicity
      1. Separate Worlds

2. Prison Segregation
   a. Prisoners were placed only with those of similar race or ethnicity for first 60 days of incarceration
D. Prison Gangs and Security Threat Groups (STGs)
   a. Prison gang – a clique of inmates who join together in an organizational structure
   1. The Prevalence of Prison Gangs
      a. 11.7% in federal prisons
      b. 13.4% in state prisons
      c. 15.6% in jails
   2. Combating Prison Gangs
      a. Security Threat Group (STG) – an identifiable group of 3 or more individuals who pose a threat to the safety of other inmates or members of the correctional community
E. Prison Rape
   1. Sexual Assault Behind Bars
   2. The Psychology of Prison Rape
III. Inside a Women's Prison
A. Characteristics of Female Inmates
   a. Males outnumber females by 9 to 1
   1. A History of Abuse
   2. Other Health Problems
B. The Motherhood Problem
   1. 7 of 10 female prisoners have at least 1 minor child
C. Violence in Women's Prisons
   a. No federal maximum or medium security women's prisons
   1. Inmate-on-Inmate Violence
   2. Sexual Violence and Prison Staff
D. The Pseudo-Family
IV. Correctional Officers and Discipline
A. Rank and Duties of Correctional Officers
   a. Block officers
   b. Work detail supervisors
   c. Industrial shop and school officers
   d. Yard officers
   e. Tower guards
   f. Administrative buildings
B. Discipline
   1. Sanctioning Prisoners
   2. Use of Force
      a. Legitimate Security Interests
      b. Justified use of force by correctional officers:
         i. Self-defense
         ii. Defend safety of third person
         iii. Uphold rules of institution
         iv. Prevent crime

          v. Prevent escape
      c. The "Malicious and Sadistic" Standard
   3. Staffing Problems
V. Protecting Prisoners' Rights
      a. Hands-off doctrine – care of inmates should be left to prison officials and not the place of judges to intervene
  A. The "Hands-On' Approach
     a. *Cooper v. Pate* (1964) ended the ands-off period
   1. A Prisoner's Liberty Interest
     a. Prisoners have due process protections when being disciplined by prison institution:
        i. A fair hearing
        ii. Written notice
        iii. Opportunity to speak at hearing
        iv. Opportunity to call witnesses
        v. Written statement detailing the final decision and reasons for decision
   2. The First Amendment in Prison
  B. Limiting Prisoners' Rights
   1. Deliberate Indifference
     a. Deliberately failing to provide prisoner with basic medical care
   2. The "Purpose" Requirement
   3. "Identifiable Human Needs"
     a. Food
     b. Warmth
     c. Exercise
VI. Parole and Release from Prison
  A. Parole
   1. Based on 3 concepts:
     a. Grace
     b. Contract of consent
     c. Custody
  B. Other Types of Prison Release
   1. Mandatory Release
     a. Inmate has served the maximum amount of time on the initial sentence
   2. Pardon
     a. President or governor forgives a convict's criminal punishment
   3. Furlough
     a. Temporary release
  C. Discretionary Release
   1. Eligibility for Parole
   2. Life Without Parole
     a. Capital or first degree murder
     b. Serious offenses other than murder
     c. Habitual or repeat offender

220

3. The Parole Board
   a. Body of appointed civilians
   b. 4 basic roles:
      i. Which offender should be placed on parole
      ii. Determine conditions of parole
      iii. Discharge offender from parole
      iv. Determine revocation of parole
4. The Parole Hearing
D. The Emergence of Mandatory Release
   1. Truth-in-Sentencing
      a. Goals:
         i. Restore truth to the sentencing process
         ii. Increase the percentage of the term actually served
         iii. Control use of prison space
   2. Parole Guidelines
      a. Standards that are used in the parole process to measure the risk that a potential parolee will recidivate
E. Parole Supervision
   a. Parole has 2 meanings:
      i. Establishment of a release date
      ii. Continuing supervision of convicted felons after they have been released
   1. Conditions of Parole
   2. Parole Revocation
      a. Parolee breaks the conditions of parole, the process of withdrawing parole and returning the person to prison
   3. Parole and Due Process
   4. Limited Rights of Parolees
VII. Reentry into Society
   a. A corrections strategy designed to prepare inmates for a successful return to the community and to reduce their criminal activity after release
A. Barriers to Reentry
   1. Challenges of Release
      a. Housing
      b. Employment
   2. The Threat of Relapse
B. Promoting Desistance
   1. Preparation for Reentry Behind Bars
   2. Positive Reinforcement on Parole
      a. Work Release and Halfway Houses
         i. Work release – temporary release of convicts for purposes of employment
         ii. Halfway house – inmates placed in residential centers and allows them to reintegrate with society
      b. Second Chance Legislation

221

C. The Special Case of Sex Offenders
  1. Sex Offender Notification Laws
    a. Requires law enforcement authorities to notify people when convicted sex offenders are released into their neighborhood or community
    b. Active and Passive Notification
    c. Conditions of Release
      i. Paroled child molesters usually have the following conditions:
        01. No contact with children under 16
        02. Continue psychiatric treatment
        03. Receive permission to change residence
        04. Stay a certain distance from schools or parks where children present
        05. Cannot own toys that may be used to lure children
        06. Cannot have a job or participate in any activity that involves children
    d. Civil Confinement
      i. Practice of confining individuals against their will if they present a danger to the community
VIII. Criminal Justice in Action— A Second Look at Residency Laws

Key Terms

civil confinement (pg. 531)
"deliberate indifference" (pg. 516)
deprivation model (pg. 500)
desistance (pg. 526)
discretionary release (pg. 518)
furlough (pg. 517)
halfway house (pg. 527)
"hands off" doctrine (pg. 513)
"identifiable humans needs" (pg. 516)
mandatory release (pg. 517)
pardon (pg. 517)
parole (pg. 517)
parole board (pg. 519)
parole contract (pg. 522)
parole grant hearing (pg. 520)
parole guidelines (pg. 521)
parole revocation (pg. 523)
prisoner reentry (pg. 524)
prison gang (pg. 502)
prisonization (pg. 498)
prison segregation (pg. 502)
relative deprivation (pg. 500)

security threat group (STGs) (pg. 503)
sex offender notification law (pg. 530)
total institution (pg. 497)
work release program (pg. 527)

Special Projects

1. Identify the number of state and federal prison facilities located in your state. Briefly provide an overall description of the prison type (e.g., minimum, maximum, or supermax) and identify whether or not any of them house female offenders. Are any of the facilities private prisons?

2. What is the typical rank hierarchy or structure for the state prisons you identified above in question one, above? Does it vary from the information described in the text?

3. What parole conditions would be considered typical for federal inmates? Use popular media or government sources to locate the information. Identify your resources and use current information.

Practice Test

True-False

_____1.   Relative deprivation theory holds that inmate aggression happens when the inmate thinks that his or her usual freedoms have been eliminated.

_____2.   Prison rape is primarily sexual rather than violent.

_____3.   Women's prisons have as much physical aggression as men's prisons.

_____4.   There are no federal maximum- or medium-security prisons for women.

_____5.   Prison violence consists of mostly inmate-on-inmate violence.

_____6.   The culture inside a prison is influenced by the beliefs and values of its inmate population.

_____7.   Paroled sex offenders face the same parole conditions as other offenders.

_____8.   Parole is a form of discretionary release.

_____9.   The officers with the least seniority in the prison are usually
             assigned as yard officers.

_____10.   The Supreme Court operated under a hands-off doctrine regarding
             inmates' rights prior to the 1960s.

_____11.   When an inmate has served all of his or her time (minus any
             adjustments for good time credits) the inmate is eligible for
             mandatory release.

_____12.   The release conditions imposed upon a sex offender often include
             a prohibition on owning toys that could appeal to children.

Multiple Choice

1. Which one is NOT associated with the concept of a total institution?
        a. Inmates are not free to leave
        b. Aspects of daily life are tightly controlled
        c. Schedules must be followed
        d. Inmates may leave for educational and employment opportunities

2. When inmates develop argot, they have essentially created their own
        a. language.
        b. currency.
        c. underground economy.
        d. social code.

3. Inmate who are more comfortable within the prison than living in the free
world exhibit behaviors known as
        a. doing time.
        b. jailing.
        c. disorganized.
        d. gleaning.

4. Which one of the following is NOT a reason for violent prison behavior?
        a. Violence serves as a deterrent to being victimized
        b. Violence is used to barter for sex and other goods
        c. Violence enhances an inmate's self concept
        d. Violence reinforces an inmate's commitment to the inmates over the
        government's authority

224

5. The prisoner rights movement resulted from
    a. the 1971 Attica prison riots.
    b. the Rodney King incident involving LAPD.
    c. the 1974 uprising at the Alcatraz prison.
    d. a violent prisoner/prison guard hostage incident.

6. The typical characteristics of female prisoners are
    a. mostly Caucasian women.
    b. an age span between 35 and 44 years of age.
    c. incarcerated for mostly non-violent crimes.
    d. a history of gainful employment and solid family relations.

7. The "safest" assignment for a correctional guard is
    a. yard officer.
    b. work detail officer.
    c. tower guard.
    d. block officer.

8. All of the following apply to inmate due process (during discipline) EXCEPT
    a. the right to appeal.
    b. the opportunity to speak at the discipline hearing.
    c. the right to be represented by an attorney.
    d. the right to have seven days notice prior to any discipline hearing.

9. Who is responsible to decide which offenders should be paroled and the conditions of parole?
    a. Parole board
    b. Warden
    c. Governor
    d. Civilian review board

10. Which one is NOT a mechanism for an inmate's release from prison?
    a. Pardon
    b. Parole
    c. Absolution
    d. Furlough

11. Life without parole is reserved for all of the following EXCEPT:
    a. habitual offenders.
    b. those convicted of capital murder.
    c. those convicted of serious offenses other than murder.
    d. those convicted of non-violent offenses.

12. "Truth-in-sentencing" seeks to
    a. force inmates to serve at least 50% of their time.
    b. force inmates to serve at least 75% of their time.
    c. force inmates to serve at least 85% of their time.
    d. force inmates to serve 100% of their time.

13. Programs that allow inmates to obtain employment during the day and return to the facility at night are called
    a. parole programs.
    b. halfway house programs.
    c. work release programs.
    d. furlough programs.

14. Parolees must remain on parole until
    a. they successfully complete one year of supervision.
    b. they successfully complete five years of supervision.
    c. they fulfill the remainder of their original sentence.
    d. the parole board determines they are no longer a risk to society.

15. Which one is not associated with an inmate's official attempt to renter society?
    a. Prison survival is not compatible with goods citizenship.
    b. Adjustment to new technologies is challenging.
    c. Adjustment to the changes in social attitudes and behaviors.
    d. Released inmates often encounter problems trying to contact their parole officer for guidance.

16. Which case officially ended the "hands-off" period?
    a. *Estelle v. Gamble*
    b. *Cooper v. Pate*
    c. *Commonwealth v. Ruffin*
    d. *Wolf v. McDonnell*

17. Laws allowing the government to keep sex offenders incarcerated even beyond the conclusion of their full prison term are known as
    a. mental health confinement.
    b. criminal confinement.
    c. civil confinement.
    d. administrative confinement.

18. Among female inmates, sex is often considered to be
    a. a sign of aggression.
    b. an expression of homosexuality.
    c. an attempt to reconstruct a traditional family structure.
    d. taboo.

19. Which one is not generally a condition placed on released sex offenders?
    a. No contact with children under the age of sixteen
    b. Must succumb to psychiatric evaluation
    c. Prohibited from possessing toys that children may find attractive
    d. Must remain gainfully employed

20. Prisoner mail may be censored if
    a. the inmate is in solitary confinement.
    b. the warden obtains a warrant to "search" it.
    c. if it is necessary to maintain facility security.
    d. if approved by the assistant warden or warden.

21. Which of the following is an example of a short-term temporary release from incarceration?
    a. Probation
    b. Parole
    c. Furlough
    d. Pardon

Fill in the Blank

1. The idea that the least advantaged member of free society should lead a better existence than any person living in jail or prison is known as the principle of _____.

2. The process by which an inmate learns the norms and values of the prison population is _____.

3. Female inmates often join tightly-knit cliques that mimic a traditional
_____.

4. _____guards are corrections officers assigned to watch over the facility in silent isolated posts.

5. Correctional officers often report that _____inmates is the most difficult aspect of the job.

6. Inmates who are trying to prove their Eighth Amendment rights were violated must be able to show the _____standard was the cause of the violation.

7. A temporary short term release from prison for vocational training or other personal reasons is known as a _____.

8. The group of civilians that decides if an inmate should be granted conditional release is _____.

9. Community residential facilities used to house paroled inmates are known as _____.

10. _____ programs consist of activities and programming to prepare released inmates for safe return to the community.

11. A situation where a group of prisoners are beyond institutional control for a significant amount of time is known as a _____.

12. Sex offender notification laws require _____ to notify the community upon an offender's release.

Short Essays

1. Explain the concept of prison as a total institution.

2. Describe the possible patterns of inmate behavior which are driven by the inmate's personality and values.

3. Indicate some of the reasons for violent behavior in prisons.

4. List and briefly explain the six general job categories among correctional officers.

5. Contrast the hands-off doctrine of prisoner law with the hands-on approach.

6. Contrast probation, parole, mandatory release, pardon, and furlough.

7. Describe truth-in-sentencing laws and their goals.

8. Describe typical conditions of parole.

9. Explain the goal of prisoner reentry programs.

10. Indicate typical conditions for release of a paroled child molester.

Answer Key

True-False:
1. T, see pg. 500, LO3
2. F, see pg. 505, LO3
3. F, see pg. 507, LO2
4. T, see pg. 507, LO2
5. T, see pg. 500, LO3
6. F, see pg. 497, LO1
7. F, see pgs. 529-530, LO10
8. T, see pg. 518, LO8
9. T, see pg. 510, LO4
10. T, see pg. 513, LO5
10. T, see pg. 521, LO6
10. T, see pg. 531, LO10

Multiple Choice:
1. d, see pg. 497, LO1
2. a, see pg. 497, LO1
3. b, see pg. 499, LO2
4. d, see pg. 500, LO3
5. a, see pg. 501, LO3
6. c, see pg. 506, LO2
7. c, see pg. 510, LO4
8. c, see pg. 514, LO5
9. b, see pg. 519, LO6
10. c, see pg. 517, LO6
11. d, see pg. 519, LO6
12. c, see pg. 521, LO7
13. c, see pg. 527, LO9
14. c, see pg. 523, LO8
15. d, see pg. 525, LO9
16. b, see pg. 513, LO5
17. c, see pg. 531, LO10
18. c, see pg. 508, LO2
19. d, see pg. 531, LO10
20. c, see pg. 515, LO5
21. c, see pg. 517, LO6

Fill in the Blank:
1. least eligibility, see pg. 496, LO1
2. prisonization, see pg. 498, LO2
3. family, see pg. 508, LO4
4. tower, see pg. 510, LO4
5. disciplining, see pg. 511, LO4
6. deliberate indifference,
   see pg. 516, LO5
7. furlough, see pg. 517, LO6
8. parole board,
   see pg. 519, LO6
9. halfway houses,
   see pg. 527, LO8
10. reentry, see pg. 524, LO9
11. riot, see pg. 501, LO3
12. law enforcement,
   see pgs. 529-530, LO10

Short Essays:
1. See pg. 497, LO1
2. See pgs. 498-499, LO2
3. See pg. 500, LO3
4. See pgs. 510-511, LO4
5. See pgs. 513-514, LO5
6. See pgs. 517-518, LO6
7. See pg. 521, LO7
8. See pg. 522, LO8
9. See pg. 524, LO9
10. See pgs. 530-531, LO10

THE JUVENILE JUSTICE SYSTEM

OUTLINE

Learning Objectives

After reading this chapter, you should be able to:

LO1: Describe the child-saving movement and its relationship to the doctrine of *parens patriae.*

LO2: List the four major differences between juvenile courts and adult courts.

LO3: Identify and briefly describe the single most important Supreme Court case with respect to juvenile justice.

LO4: List the factors that normally determine what police do with juvenile offenders.

LO5: Describe the four primary stages of pretrial juvenile justice procedure.

LO6: Explain the distinction between an adjudicatory hearing and a disposition hearing.

LO7: List the four categories of residential treatment programs.

LO8: Describe the one variable that always correlates highly with juvenile crime rates.

LO9: Indicate some reasons why youths join gangs.

Chapter Outline

I. The Evolution of American Juvenile Justice
    A. The Child-Saving Movement
        1. Parens Patriae
            a. The state not only has a right but a duty to care for children who are neglected, delinquent, or in some other way disadvantaged
    B. The Illinois Juvenile Court
        1. First in the Nation, 1899
        2. Different from adult courts:
            a. Terminology
            b. No adversarial relationship
            c. Confidentiality
    C. Juvenile Delinquency
        1. Delinquents versus Status Offenders
            a. Status offenders – juvenile who has been found to have engaged in behavior deemed unacceptable for those under a statutorily defined age
            b. Juvenile delinquency – behavior that is illegal under federal or state law that has been committed by a person who is under an age limit specified by statute
    D. Constitutional Protections and the Juvenile Court
        1. *Kent v. United States*
            a. Due process rights to juveniles
        2. *In re Gault*
            a. Entitled to same due process rights as adults
            b. *In re Winship*

234

      c. *Breed v. Jones*

      d. McKeiver v. Pennsylvania

II. Determining Delinquency Today

    A. The Age Question

      1. The Common Law Response

        a. Child under 7 considered to lack *mens rea*

      2. The Modern Response

        a. Generally no age restriction

    B. The Culpability Question

III. First Contact: Delinquents and the Police

    A. Police Discretion and Juvenile Crime

      1. Low-Visibility Decision making

        a. Police consider the following factors:

          i. Nature of offense

          ii. Past history with system

          iii. Setting in which offense took place

          iv. Ability of parents

          v. Attitude of offender

          vi. Offender's race and gender

      2. Arrests of Minority Youths

      3. Failing the "Attitude Test"

    B. Juveniles and the Constitution

      1. Searches and Students

        a. *New Jersey v. T.L.O.*

          i. Reasonable suspicion

      2. *Miranda* Warnings

      3. The Right to a Jury Trial

IV. Pretrial Procedures in Juvenile Justice

    A. Intake

      1. Intake – Following referral of a juvenile to juvenile court by a police officer or other concerned party

      2. Filing a Petition

        a. Petition – the document filed with a juvenile court alleging that the juvenile is a delinquent or a status offender and asking the court to either hear the case or transfer it to an adult court

    B. Pretrial Diversion

      1. Probation

      2. Treatment and Aid

      3. Restitution

    C. Transfer to Adult Court

      1. Methods of Transfer

        a. Judicial Waiver – process in which the juvenile judge, based on the facts of the case at hand, decides that the alleged offender should be transferred to adult court

        b. Automatic Transfer – process by which a juvenile is transferred to adult court as a matter of state law in some states

      c. Prosecutorial Waiver – procedure used in situations in which juvenile and adult courts have concurrent jurisdiction over certain offenses

    2. Transfer and Adult Corrections

  D. Detention

        i.   Temporary custody of a juvenile in a secure facility after a petition has been filed and before the adjudicatory process begins

        a. Detention Hearing – a hearing to determine whether a juvenile should be detained or continue to be detained

        b. 3 issues in hearing:

            i.   Whether child poses a danger to the community

           ii. Whether the child will return for adjudication process

           iii. Whether detention will provide protection for the child

        c. *Schall v. Martin*

V. Juveniles on Trial

  A. Adjudication

    1. Adjudication Hearing

      a. The process through which a juvenile court determines whether there is sufficient evidence to support the initial petition

  B. Disposition

    1. Disposition Hearing

      a. Juvenile judge or officer decides the appropriate punishment for a youth found to be delinquent or a status offender

    2. Sentencing Juveniles

      a. A report prepared during the disposition process that provides the judge with relevant background material to aid in the disposition decision

    3. Judicial Discretion

VI. Juvenile Corrections

    1. Graduated sanctions – delinquent or status offender should received a punishment that matches in seriousness the severity of the wrongdoing

  A. Juvenile Probation

  B. Confining Juveniles

      a. About 95,000 are incarcerated in U.S.

    1. Nonsecure Confinement

      a. Residential Treatment Program

        i.   Facility for juveniles whose offenses are not deemed serious enough to warrant incarceration in a training school

          01. Foster care programs

          02. Group homes

          03. Family group homes

          04. Rural programs

    2. Secure Confinement

      a. Boot Camps – Juveniles sent to a secure confinement facility modeled on military basic training camps instead of prison or jail

  b. Training Schools – Correctional institution for juveniles found to be delinquent or status offenders

 C. Aftercare

VII. Trends in Juvenile Delinquency

 A. Delinquency by the Numbers

 B. Is juvenile Crime Leveling Off?

  1. Violent Crime Trends

  2. Reasons for the Decline

   a. Crack Decline

   b. Zero Tolerance

   c. Quality of Life Crimes

 C. Girls in the Juvenile Justice System

  1. A Growing Presence

  2. Family-Based Delinquency

 D. School Violence

  1. Security Efforts

  2. The Bully Problem

VIII. Factors in Juvenile Delinquency

 A. The Age–Crime Relationship

  1. Aging Out – criminal activity declines with age

  2. Age of Onset – the age at which a juvenile for exhibits delinquent behavior, the earlier the age, the greater chance they will become a career offender

 B. Substance Abuse

  1. Downward Trends

  2. Continued Abuse

 C. Child Abuse and Neglect

  1. Child Abuse – physical or emotional damage on a child

  2. Neglect – deprivations of love, shelter, food, and proper care

 D. Gangs

   a. Youth gangs – group of 3 or more persons who

    i. Self-identify themselves as an entity separate from the community by special clothing, vocabulary, hand signals, and names

    ii. Engage in criminal activity

  1. Who Joins Gangs?

   a. Average 17-18 years of age

   b. 49% Hispanic

   c. 35% African American

   d. 9% white

   e. 7% other ethnic groups

  2. Why Do Youths Join Gangs?

   a. Linked with status in community

  3. Gangs and Crime

 E. Guns

IX. Keeping Juvenile Delinquency under Control

A. Transfer to Adult Court
   B. Social Control Regulation
      1. Curfews
      2. Parental Responsibility Statutes
   C. Community Programs
X. Criminal Justice in Action—Life without Parole for Juveniles

Key Terms

Adjudicatory hearing (pg. 562)
Aftercare (pg. 563)
Age of onset (pg. 568)
Aging out (pg. 568)
Automatic transfer (pg. 456)
Boot camp (pg. 563)
Child abuse (pg. 570)
Child neglect (pg. 570)
Detention (pg. 557)
Detention hearing (pg. 557)
Disposition hearing (pg. 558)
Graduated sanctions (pg. 560)
Intake (pg. 554)
Judicial waiver (pg. 555)
Juvenile delinquency (pg. 545)
Low-visibility decision making (pg. 550)
Parens patriae (pg. 543)
Petition (pg. 554)
Predisposition report (pg. 559)
Prosecutorial waiver (pg. 556)
Referral (pg. 550)
Residential treatment programs (pg. 561)
Status offender (pg. 544)
Training schools (pg. 563)
Youth gangs (pg. 570)

Special Projects

1. Research juvenile crime in your state. What county has the largest percentage of juvenile crime? Identity (if possible) the types of crimes that seem to be the most prevalent (violent or non-violent and specific crime class). Did any of the information surprise you? Have juvenile crime rates been increasing or decreasing?

2. Research a significant criminal case (e.g., case received a significant amount of media attention, case had a unique victim, offender's age) involving a juvenile offender that occurred within your state. What circumstances make this case significant? Identify the case and its outcome, and the age of the offender at the time of the crime. Summarize the case in a short report.

3. What juvenile programs does your local community offer? Do you feel that such programs could discourage criminal behavior in young people? Of the programs you identified which seems to be the most popular and why? Interview someone involved with the program(s) and ask their opinion as to how valuable the programs are as a crime deterrent.

Practice Test

True-False

_____1.   Juveniles are most commonly transferred to adult court through juvenile waiver.

_____2.   Because police discretion is controversial in nature, it is strongly regulated and seldom used in determining how to manage a juvenile offender in the criminal justice system.

_____3.   *Roper v. Simmons* prohibits the execution of offenders who were under age eighteen when they did their crime.

_____4.   Low-visibility decision making is inherent in police handling of juveniles.

_____5.   With regard to search and seizure by school administrators, the court has justified a lower standard of proof for searching students and school lockers. This revised standard is a by-product of the *in loco parentis* doctrine.

_____6.   The age of a youthful offender has been identified as the primary or key variable associated with juvenile crime rates.

_____7.   "Graduated sanctions" are sanctions that are proportionate to the crime. In other words, the punishment should fit the crime.

_____8.   Juvenile probation officers are expected to take the role of mentor.

_____9.   Training schools differ greatly from adult prisons and jails.

_____10.   As a result of the U.S. Supreme Court's ruling in *Gault,* juvenile courts are required to impanel a twelve person jury for juvenile felony criminal trials.

_____11.   Juvenile girls are becoming more and more visible in the juvenile criminal justice system.

_____12.   Many criminal charges against female delinquents stem from incidents of family based delinquency such as domestic violence.

Multiple Choice

1. Which of the following is true of juvenile courts?
    a. Juries are impaneled
    b. The justice process is adversarial in nature just like adult court
    c. Juveniles court actions are public and as such there is no confidentiality attached to these records
    d. Juvenile courts utilize different terminology than adult courts

2. Which court case has been identified as the most significant in terms of its overall impact on the American juvenile justice system?
    a. *Kent v. United States*
    b. *In re Gault*
    c. *In re Winship*
    d. *Breed v. Jones*

3. Which due process right was NOT a part of the U.S. Supreme Court's *In re Gault* ruling?
    a. Juveniles have a right to advance notice of charges
    b. Juveniles have a right to counsel
    c. Juveniles are entitled to full due process
    d. Juveniles have a right to public trials before their peers

4. With regard to how police officers manage juveniles; which one is NOT identified in the text as a factor that would affect police discretion (decision making)?
    a. The offender's past history
    b. Whether or not the juvenile is illiterate
    c. The willingness of the parents (responsible guardian) to take disciplinary action
    d. The offender's overall attitude

5. The first stage of juvenile pretrial procedures is
    a. intake.
    b. diversion.
    c. waiver.
    d. detention.

6. What overall category does juvenile diversion belong to?
    a. Probation
    b. Training school
    c. Parole
    d. Residential treatment

7. Juveniles can be transferred to adult court by way of legislative mandate or
    a. judicial waiver.
    b. indictment.
    c. direct placement.
    d. judicial inquest.

8. A court's decision to detain a juvenile is generally based on all of the following EXCEPT
    a. the danger the child poses to the community.
    b. the probability of the child's return for adjudication.
    c. the probability of protecting the child.
    d. the amount of media attention the case receives.

9. What do juvenile justice courts have in common with their adult court counterparts?
    a. The right to a jury trial exists
    b. Hearings must be open to the public and press
    c. The burden of proof is the same--beyond a reasonable doubt
    d. The process is adversarial in nature

10. The case of *Roper v. Simmons* is significant to the juvenile justice system because
    a. it afforded juveniles protection from self-incrimination.
    b. it provided juveniles adjudication by a jury of peers.
    c. it prohibited capital punishment for juveniles under the age of eighteen.
    d. it provided protection from unlawful search and seizure on school controlled property.

11. Which one is NOT associated with the juvenile justice system?
    a. Defense attorneys
    b. Plea bargaining
    c. Parental or guardian involvement
    d. Public trials

12. The primary consideration in juvenile sentencing is the
    a. needs of the child.
    b. needs of the family.
    c. needs of the community.
    d. court's available resources and its ability to properly handle the case.

13. Residential treatment programs include all of the following components
EXCEPT
    a. foster care.
    b. family group homes.
    c. orphanages.
    d. group homes.

14. In the juvenile system, parole is referred to as
    a. aftercare.
    b. probation.
    c. day treatment.
    d. parole.

15. Which facility type houses approximately 12-15 youths and employs a
professional staff to provide treatment, counseling, and rehabilitation services?
    a. Foster care programs
    b. Group homes
    c. Family group homes
    d. Rural programs

16. Which one was NOT identified in the text as a school based juvenile
delinquency *risk factor*?
    a. Academic failure
    b. School uniforms
    c. Labeling by teachers
    d. Discipline problems

17. Which one was NOT identified in the text as a community based juvenile
delinquency *risk factor*?
    a. Family members in gangs
    b. Delinquent friends and associates
    c. Alcohol use
    d. Being socially introverted

18. Which one was NOT identified in the text as a peer based juvenile
delinquency *risk factor*?
    a. Poorly educated peers
    b. Delinquent peers
    c. Peers who use drugs
    d. Positive peer pressure

242

19. Which one is NOT identified in the text as a reason for juvenile gang membership?
   a. Juveniles join because they gain status in the community
   b. Juveniles join gangs in order to protect themselves from other gangs
   c. Juveniles join gangs for excitement
   d. Juveniles join gangs because of religious pressure to conform

20. Which one is NOT generally associated with youth gangs?
   a. Special clothing
   b. Special names
   c. Special symbols
   d. Formal clubhouses

21. Gang members are more likely to be drawn together by commonality of
   a. race.
   b. religion.
   c. social and economic status.
   d. ethnic culture.

22. Social control regulation calls for
   a. transfer of a juvenile offender to adult court.
   b. the enactment of parental responsibility statutes.
   c. establishing community based programming.
   d. stricter penalties for the youthful offender.

23. The deprivation of food, clothing, shelter and proper care is better known as
   a. parental inadequacy.
   b. child abuse.
   c. child neglect.
   d. poverty.

24. Which one was NOT identified in the text as an overall juvenile delinquency *risk factor*?
   a. Broken home environment
   b. Learning disability
   c. Poverty and a lack of economic opportunity
   d. Teacher reinforcement and support

25. Child-saving organizations convinced local legislatures to pass laws allowing the organizations to take control of children who
   a. were performing poorly in school.
   b. exhibited criminal tendencies or had been neglected by their parents.
   c. were suffering from contagious diseases and posed a public health risk.
   d. exhibited signs of intellectual superiority or genius.

243

Fill in the Blank

1. The _____doctrine posits that the state not only has a right, but a duty, to care for neglected or otherwise disadvantaged children.

2. The first court specifically for juveniles was established in _____ in Illinois.

3. A juvenile who has been found to have engaged in behavior which is unacceptable because of a statutorily designated age is identified as a _____ offender.

4. Behavior that is illegal under federal of state law that has been committed by a person under an age limit specified by statute is termed juvenile _____.

5. The process of removing low-risk offenders from the formal juvenile justice system and placing then in other programs is _____.

6. The theory that criminal activity declines with age is called _____.

7. Most theorists identify _____ as the single most consistent factor related to juvenile delinquency.

8. Child _____ is the deprivation of love, shelter, food, and proper care.

9. Child _____ is physical or emotional damage to a child.

10. The process by which a court official decides to file a petition, release a juvenile, or place the juvenile under some form of supervision is known as _____.

11. The process of _____ transfer occurs when a juvenile is transferred to adult court because of legal mandate (state law).

12. During the course of a _____ hearing, a juvenile judge or judicial official decides the appropriate punishment for a juvenile offender.

244

Short Essays

1. Describe the child-saving movement and its relationship to the doctrine of *parens patriae*.

2. List the four major differences between juvenile courts and adult courts.

3. Identify and briefly describe the single most important Supreme Court case with respect to juvenile justice.

4. List the factors that normally determine what police do with juvenile offenders.

5. Describe the four primary stages of pretrial juvenile justice procedure.

6. Explain the distinction between an adjudicatory hearing and a disposition hearing.

7. List the four categories of residential treatment programs.

8. Describe the one variable that always correlates highly with juvenile crime rates.

9. Indicate some reasons why youths join gangs.

10. Gangs seem to have been part of humanity since our beginnings. What is inherently wrong with a gang? Justify your answer with an explanatory essay. Draw on information from this graph, which shows the percentage of juvenile convictions for different crimes. Also draw on what you have learned throughout the chapter.

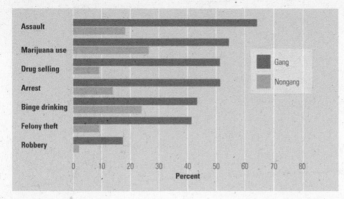

Answer Key

True-False:
1. T, see pg. 555, LO5
2. F, see pg. 550, LO4
3. T, see pg. 549, LO3
4. T, see pg. 550, LO4
5. T, see pg. 552, LO4
6. T, see pg. 568, LO8
7. T, see pg. 560, LO7
8. T, see pg. 561, LO6
9. F, see pg. 563, LO7
10. F, see pg. 546, LO2
11. T, see pg. 565, LO8
12. T, see pg. 566, LO8

Multiple Choice:
1. d, see pg. 544, LO2
2. b, see pg. 545, LO3
3. d, see pg. 545, LO3
4. b, see pg. 550, LO4
5. a, see pg. 554, LO5
6. a, see pg. 555, LO5
7. a, see pg. 555, LO5
8. d, see pg. 557, LO5
9. c, see pg. 559, LO6
10. c, see pg. 549, LO3
11. d, see pg. 559, LO6
12. a, see pg. 558, LO6
13. c, see pg. 561, LO7
14. a, see pg. 563, LO7
15. b, see pg. 561, LO7
16. b, see pg. 568, LO8
17. d, see pg. 568, LO8
18. d, see pg. 568, LO8
19. d, see pgs. 570-571, LO9
20. d, see pg. 570, LO9
21. c, see pg. 571, LO9
22. b, see pg. 573, LO4
23. c, see pg. 570, LO8
24. d, see pg. 568, LO8
25. b, see pg. 543, LO1

Fill in the Blank:
1. *parens patriae*, see pg. 543, LO1
2. 1899, see pg. 544, LO2
3. status, see pg. 544, LO2
4. delinquency, see pg. 545, LO2
5. diversion, see pg. 555, LO5
6. aging-out, see pg. 568, LO8
7. age, see pg. 568, LO8
8. neglect, see pg. 570, LO8
9. abuse, see pg. 570, LO8
10. intake, see pg. 554, LO5
11. automatic, see pg. 556, LO5
12. disposition, see pg. 558, LO6

Short Essays:
1. See pgs. 543-544, LO1
2. See pg. 544, LO2
3. See pgs. 545-546, LO3
4. See pg. 546, LO4
5. See pgs. 554-557, LO5
6. See pgs. 557-558, LO6
7. See pg. 561, LO7
8. See pgs. 568-569, LO8
9. See pgs. 570-572, LO9
10. See pgs. 570-572, LO9

HOMELAND SECURITY

OUTLINE

Learning Objectives

After reading this chapter, you should be able to:

LO1:   Identify five important trends in international terrorism.
LO2:   Describe the several strains of domestic terrorism.
LO3:   Compare WMDs and CBERN.
LO4:   Explain why the Antiterrorism and Effective Death Penalty Act of 1996 (AEDPA) is an important legal tool against terrorists.
LO5:   Describe the primary goals of an intelligence agency and indicate how it differs from an agency that focuses solely on law enforcement.
LO6:   Explain how American law enforcement agencies have used "preventive policing" to combat terrorism.
LO7:   List the primary duties of first responders following a terrorist attack or other catastrophic event.
LO8:   Describe the differences between criminal law and immigration law with regard to suspected terrorists.
LO9:   Explain how the Patriot Act has made it easier for federal agents to conduct searches during terrorism investigations.

Chapter Outline

I.   An Introduction to Terrorism
  a.   Nonstate Actor – an entity that plays a role in international affairs but does not represent any established state or nation
  A.   Defining Terrorism
    a.   FBI definition – the unlawful use of force or violence against persons or property to intimidate or coerce a government, the civilian population, or any segment thereof, in further of political or social objectives
  B.   The Global Context of Terrorism
    1.   Osama bin Laden and al Qaeda
    a.   al Qaeda roughly translated to mean "the base"has 2 meanings:
      i.   Diffuse, general anti-Western global social movement
      ii.   Specific organization responsible for the September 11 attacks and numerous other terrorist activities over the past 2 decades
    b.   Jihad refers to:
      i.   The struggle against the evil in oneself
      ii.   The struggle against the evil outside of oneself
      iii.   The struggle against nonbelivers
    2.   al Qaeda versus the United States
  C.   Trends in International Terrorism
    1.   Passing the Torch
    2.   Challenges for the Future

a. Terrorists have developed more efficient methods of financing their operations

b. Terrorists have developed more efficient organizations

c. Terrorists have exploited new communications technology to mount global campaigns

D. Domestic Terrorism – Acts of terrorism that take place within the territorial jurisdiction of the U.S. without direct foreign involvement

1. The Radicalization of Religion

2. The Radicalization of Politics

a. Ecoterrorism – a movement that commits acts of violence, sabotage, or property damage motivated by a desire to protect the environment

i. Animal Liberation Front (ALF)

ii. Earth Liberation Front (ELF)

II. The Terrorist Threat

A. The Weaponry of Terrorism

a. Weapons of Mass Destruction (WMD) – nuclear, radiological, chemical, or biological weapons that have the capacity to cause large numbers of casualties or do significant property damage

1. Types of WMDs

a. Biological weapon

i. Any living organism used to intentionally harm or kill adversaries in war or targets of terrorist attacks

b. Chemical weapon

i. Any weapon that uses a manufactured chemical to harm or kill adversaries in war or targets of terrorist attacks

c. Nuclear weapons

i. An explosive device that derives its massive destructive power from the release of nuclear energy

d. Radiation

i. Harmful energy that is transmitted outward from it source through rays, waves, or particles following the detonation of a nuclear device

2. Conventional Explosives

a. IEDs – Improvised explosive devices:

i. Explosive charges created using nonmilitary or nontraditional components, often used by terrorists or other nonstate actors without access to standard weapons training

b. CBERN – Chemical, Biological, Explosive, Radiological, Nuclear

c. RDDs – Radiological Dispersion Device

B. The Incidence of WMDs

III. The Homeland Security Response

A. The Antiterrorism and Effective Death Penalty Act of 1996

B. The Patriot Act

1. "Leveling the Playing Field"

a. Selected aspects:

251

         i. Relaxes restrictions on information sharing between U.S. law enforcement agencies and other government agencies
        ii. Crime to knowingly harbor a terrorist
      iii. Greater freedom in seizing e-mail records
      iv. Tripled number of some federal agents
       v. Eliminated statute of limitations for some terrorist related crimes
   2. Renewing the Patriot Act
C. The Department of Homeland Security
   1. The Office of the Secretary
   2. The Agencies of the DHS:
      a. CBP
      b. ICE
      c. USSS
      d. U.S. Coast Guard
      e. TSA
      f. USCIS
      g. FEMA
D. Federal Agencies Outside the DHS
   1. The FBI
   2. Intelligence Agencies – primarily concerned with gathering information about potential criminal or terrorist events in order to prevent them
      a. Rely on the following:
         i. Electronic surveillance
        ii. Human-source collection
      iii. Open-source collection
      iv. Intelligence sharing
       v. Counterintelligence
      b. CIA – responsible for collecting and coordinating foreign intelligence operations
      c. NSA – responsible for protecting U.S. government communications and producing intelligence by monitoring foreign communications
E. International Counterterrorism Efforts
   1. Cooperative Efforts
   2. Jurisdictional Restraints
   3. Extraditing Terrorist Suspects
IV. Counterterrorism Challenges and Strategies
  A. Preventive Policing
   1. Taking no Chances
   2. Informants and Intelligence
  B. Three Models: Criminal Justice, Intelligence, and Military
      a. The First Attack on New York
      b. The Intelligence and Military Models
         i. Reforming the FBI
        ii. Military Solutions
      c. New Initiatives
  C. Emergency Preparedness and Response

1. Preparedness and Response
   a. Preparedness – actions taken by governments to prepare for large-scale catastrophic events such as terrorist attacks or environmental disasters
   b. First responders – Firefighters, police officers, and emergency medical technicians responsible for:
      i. Securing the scene of the incident by maintaining order
      ii. Rescuing and treating any injured civilians
      iii. Containing and suppressing fires or other hazardous conditions that have resulted from the incident
      iv. Retrieving those who have been killed
2. Preparedness Concerns

V. Border Security
   A. Immigration Law Basics
      a. Alien – A person who is not a citizen of the country in which he or she is found and therefore may not enjoy the same rights and protections as a citizen of that country
      1. Visa Requirements
         a. Visa – Official authorization allowing a person to travel to and within the issuing country
      2. The Role of Immigration Law
   B. Regulated Ports of Entry
      1. Legal Loopholes
      2. Illegal Presence
   C. Unregulated Ports of Entry
      1. A Logistical Nightmare
      2. Stemming the Flow
      3. Terrorist Crossings

VI. The Double-Edged Sword: Security versus Civil Liberties
   A. The First Freedoms: Speech and Religion
      1. Terrorist Incitement
         a. Promoting Jihad
         b. Online Support
      2. Cultural Profiling
   B. Searches, Surveillance, and Security
      1. The Patriot Act and Searches
      2. The Patriot Act and Surveillance
      3. The NSA and Warrantless Wiretaps
   C. Due Process and Indefinite Detention
      1. The Bush Administration's Strategy
         a. Unlawful Combatants
            i. A person who takes part in armed hostilities but who does not belong to the armed forces of a sovereign nation and, therefore, is not afforded protection under the Geneva Conventions
         b. Military Tribunals

i.   A court that is operated by the military rather than the criminal
                         justice system and is presided over by military officers rather
                         than judges
                c. The Supreme Court Responds
                d. Changing Course
                     i.   Closing GTMO
                     ii. Ending Military Tribunals
VII.   Criminal Justice in Action—Interrogating Terrorists

Key Terms

Alien (pg. 610)
Antiterrorism and Effective Death Penalty Act (AEDPA) (pg. 597)
Biological weapon (pg. 594)
Central Intelligence Agency (CIA) (pg. 601)
Chemical Weapon (pg. 594)
Domestic Terrorism (pg.592)
Eco-terrorism (pg. 593)
First responders (pg. 609)
Improvised explosive devices (IEDs) (pg. 596)
Infrastructure (pg. 600)
Intelligence agency (pg. 601)
Military tribunal (pg. 621)
National Security Agency (NSA) (pg. 601)
Nonstate actor (pg. 587)
Nuclear weapon (pg. 594)
Patriot Act (pg. 598)
Preparedness (pg. 609)
Radiation (pg. 594)
Unlawful combatant (pg. 621)
Visa (pg. 610)
Weapons of mass destruction (WMDs) (pg. 594)

Special Projects

1. Research the concept of 'homeland security" in your local area. What changes
have been made by emergency responders since the 9 /11 attacks? Are the
changes tied to the Homeland Security Act of 2002? Identify the changes. In your
opinion have the changes enhanced overall public safety?

2. Identify a large scale critical incident that occurred in your home state. Did the incident require first responders as well as local, state and federal responders? Was FEMA involved? In your opinion was the response appropriate to the scale of the incident? Were there any problems with how the overall incident was managed?

3. Identify a local jurisdiction that has conducted an emergency preparedness drill (i.e., a homeland security drill). Prepare a short report on the drill. What type of incident was managed in the drill? What agencies responded and were multiple disciplines involved? What problems or inadequacies were discovered as a result of the drill? How was the drill funded? Did anything unusual happen during the drill (i.e., public scare, unexpected injury, equipment malfunction)?

Practice Test

True-False

_____1.　　*Jihad* has been translated as referring *to* "holy war".

_____2.　　Domestic terrorism is the term assigned to any terror attack that occurs on United States' soil.

_____3.　　The most active strain of domestic terrorism is eco-terrorism.

_____4.　　There is no connection between the issues of illegal immigration and terrorism.

_____5.　　Anthrax is considered to be both a biological weapon and a weapon of mass destruction (WMD).

_____6.　　IED's manufactured by amateurs are the dominant type of weapon used in terrorist type attacks.

_____7.　　The FBI is the lead agency in the Department of Homeland Security.

_____8.　　Under the criminal justice model, terrorism is treated like any other criminal offense.

_____9.　　Ports of entry into the United States are regulated by the FBI with an emphasis on immigration law.

_____10.　　In a military tribunal, a defendant does not have a right to trial by jury.

Multiple Choice

1. Osama bin Laden's al Qaeda group is believed to have originated in
    a. Iraq.
    b. Saudi Arabia.
    c. Afghanistan.
    d. Pakistan.

2. Which one has NOT been identified in the text as a trend or characteristic of modern terrorism?
    a. Terrorist attacks are becoming more violent.
    b. Terrorists are becoming more organized.
    c. The number of nations being controlled by terror groups is rising at a significant pace.
    d. Terrorists are getting better at mounting global campaigns.

3. The term *Jihad* means
    a. the base.
    b. a series of struggles.
    c. holy war.
    d. a group of religious extremists who have become terrorists.

4. Which act has been identified as the worst act of American domestic terrorism?
    a. The 9 /11 attack(s)
    b. The anthrax mailings
    c. The bombing at Olympic Park in Georgia
    d. The bombing of a federal building in Oklahoma City

5. The most active form of domestic terrorism today is
    a. eco-terrorism.
    b. al Qaeda.
    c. the pro-life movement.
    d. the white supremacy movement.

6. The first-known deliberate use of a biological weapon in the United States involved
    a. sarin gas.
    b. anthrax.
    c. ricin.
    d. West Nile Virus.

7. Sarin, ricin, and cyanide are classified as
   a. chemical weapons.
   b. neurological weapons.
   c. biological weapons.
   d. radiological weapons.

8. To infiltrate homegrown terrorist cells, law enforcement today relies heavily on
   a. new legislation outlawing such groups.
   b. unmanned aerial vehicles.
   c. intelligence provided from informants and other sources.
   d. immigration law and border security.

9. The phrase "material support" was introduced as a key component of the
   a. Geneva Convention.
   b. Patriot Act.
   c. Homeland Security Act.
   d. AEDPA.

10. Which of the following was overlooked (and was excluded) as "material support" in the original legislation?
    a. Lodging
    b. Transportation and food assistance
    c. Donations to foreign terror organizations
    d. Communication devices or services (digital or otherwise)

11. Prior to 9/11, disaster management was the primary responsibility of the
    a. FEMA.
    b. FBI.
    c. Red Cross.
    d. Department of Homeland Security.

12. Which of the following agencies is NOT a part of the Department of Homeland Security?
    a. FEMA
    b. FBI
    c. TSA
    d. ICE

13. Which agency is responsible for handling the administrative or "paperwork" side of U.S. immigration?
    a. ICE
    b. CBP
    c. USCIS
    d. TSA

257

14. The process of recruiting foreign agents to collect and provide information to assist in the war against terror, is called
     a. intellectual intelligence.
     b. human-source collection.
     c. open-source collection.
     d. counterintelligence.

15. The agency responsible for analyzing communications between foreign governments and citizens is the
     a. National Security Agency.
     b. Central Intelligence Agency.
     c. Federal Bureau of Investigation.
     d. U.S. Secret Service.

16. The case of the "Liberty Seven" is representative of new challenges for the law enforcement community. These new challenges include
     a. managing toxic biological weapons.
     b. managing disaster scenes of an unprecedented scale and scope.
     c. learning to trust technology and its capabilities.
     d. preventing crimes before they occur.

17. Which agency came under significant criticism for its handling of the 9/11 attacks and the events that led to it?
     a. Department of Homeland Security
     b. Federal Emergency Management Agency
     c. National Security Agency
     d. Federal Bureau of Investigation

18. Which response model involves deploying the U.S. Military to combat terrorism?
     a. Intelligence model
     b. Criminal Justice model
     c. Military model
     d. Enemy Combatant model

19. For actions that have a significant purpose, the Patriot Act authorizes the FBI to quickly obtain warrants for (1) terrorism investigations, (2) chemical weapon investigations and, (3) computer fraud and abuse. What makes this legislation unique when compared to processes for other "routine" criminal investigations?
     a. This legislation makes obtaining a warrant really a "rubber stamp."
     b. This legislation does not require a judge or other judicial official to approve the warrant in order for it be valid---Congress will approve it.
     c. This legislation authorizes military officers to authorize warrants.
     d. This legislation does not require proof of criminal activity for a warrant to be issued.

20. Osama bin Laden's al Qaeda group has been traced back as far as the
     a. 1940s.
     b. 1950s.
     c. 1970s.
     d. 1980s.

21. Which of the following is NOT considered to be a "first responder"?
     a. U.S. Military including National Guard
     b. Police officers
     c. Firefighters
     d. Emergency medical technicians

22. Approximately how many foreign visitors arrive in the U.S. each year?
     a. 29 million
     b. 67 million
     c. 50 million
     d. 88 million

23. According to the text, critics have identified all of the following Constitutional Amendments as being strained by the Patriot Act, EXCEPT
     a. the Fourth Amendment.
     b. the Fifth Amendment.
     c. the Sixth Amendment.
     d. the Twelfth Amendment.

24. What is the difference between military tribunals and the criminal court?
     a. Tribunals do not impanel a jury
     b. Tribunals are civil courts not criminal courts
     c. Tribunals do not determine guilt or innocence
     d. Tribunals do not impose the death penalty as part of sanctioning

Fill in the Blank

1. According to the FBI, the most active and well-organized form of domestic terrorism is _____.

2. Any living organism, such as bacterium or a virus, used to intentionally harm or kill adversaries in a war is considered to be a _____ weapon.

3. A true "doomsday" terrorist attack involves _____ weapons.

4. The popular term for a radiological dispersion device is a(n) _____.

5. Currency, under AEDPA, financial services, and physical assets may be considered _____ support.

6. Prior to the 9/11 attack(s), the primary federal agency responsible for disaster management was the _____.

7. The _____ is the agency responsible for the safe operation of airline, bus, and rail services.

8. The _____ model regards terrorist activities as threats to the security of the state rather than criminal acts.

9. A(n) _____ is official authorization allowing a person to travel to and within the issuing nation.

10. A(n) _____ is not a citizen in the country in which they are found.

11. The _____ Amendment holds that no person shall be deprived of life, liberty, or property without due process of law.

12. The military plan to deal with prisoners of war was to adjudicate them by way of _____ in lieu of criminal court trial.

Short Essays

1.   Identify five important trends in international terrorism.

2. Describe the several strains of domestic terrorism.

3. Compare WMDs and CBERN.

4. Explain why the Antiterrorism and Effective Death Penalty Act of 1996 (AEDPA) is an important legal tool against terrorists.

5. Describe the primary goals of an intelligence agency and indicate how it differs from an agency that focuses solely on law enforcement.

6. Explain how American law enforcement agencies have used "preventive policing" to combat terrorism.

7. List the primary duties of first responders following a terrorist attack or other catastrophic event.

8. Describe the differences between criminal law and immigration law with regard to suspected terrorists.

9. Explain how the Patriot Act has made it easier for federal agents to conduct searches during terrorism investigations.

Answer Key

True-False:
1. F, see pg. 590, LO1
2. F, see pg. 592, LO2
3. T, see pg. 593, LO2
4. F, see pg. 610, LO8
5. T, see pg. 594, LO3
6. T, see pg. 596, LO3
7. F, see pg. 599, LO4
8. T, see pgs. 606-607, LO5
9. F, see pg. 611, LO8
10. T, see pg. 621, LO1/9

Multiple Choice:
1. c, see pg. 590, LO1
2. c, see pgs. 591-592, LO1
3. b, see pg. 590, LO1
4. d, see pg. 593, LO2
5. a, see pg. 593, LO2
6. b, see pg. 594, LO3
7. a, see pg. 595, LO2
8. c, see pg. 605, LO6
9. d, see pg. 597, LO4
10. c, see pg. 598, LO4
11. a, see pg. 598, LO4
12. b, see pg. 599, LO4
13. c, see pg. 600, LO5
14. b, see pg. 601, LO5
15. a, see pg. 601, LO5
16. d, see pg. 605, LO6
17. d, see pg. 603, LO4
18. c, see pgs. 607-608, LO6
19. d, see pg. 619, LO9
20. d, see pg. 590, LO2
21. a, see pg. 609, LO7
22. d, see pg. 611, LO8
23. d, see pg. 616, LO9
24. a, see pg. 621, LO9

Fill in the Blank:
1. eco-terrorism, see pg. 593, LO2
2. biological, see pg. 594, LO3
3. nuclear, see pg. 594, LO3
4. dirty bomb, see pg. 596, LO3
5. material support, see pg. 597, LO4
6. FEMA, see pg. 599, LO4
7. TSA, see pg. 600, LO5
8. intelligence, see pg. 607, LO6
9. VISA, see pg. 610, LO8
10. alien, see pg. 610, LO8
11. Fifth, see pg. 616, LO9
12. military tribunal, see pg. 621, LO1/9

Short Essays:
1. See pgs. 591-592, LO1
2. See pgs. 592-593, LO2
3. See pgs. 594-596, LO3
4. See pgs. 597-598, LO4
5. See pg. 601, LO5
6. See pgs. 605-606, LO6
7. See pg. 609, LO7
8. See pgs. 610-611, LO8
9. See pg. 619, LO9

CYBER CRIME AND THE FUTURE OF CRIMINAL JUSTICE

OUTLINE

Learning Objectives

After reading this chapter, you should be able to:

LO1: Distinguish cyber crime from "traditional" crime.
LO2: Indicate how the Internet has expanded opportunities for identity theft.
LO3   Explain the differences between cyberstalking and cyberbullying.
LO4: Describe the three following forms of malware: (a) botnets, (b) worms, and (c) viruses.
LO5: Explain how the Internet has contributed to piracy of intellectual property.
LO6: Outline the three major reasons why the Internet is conducive to the dissemination of child pornography.
LO7: Indicate how encryption programs protect digital data from unauthorized access.
LO8: Explain why the right to free speech on the Internet is not absolute.

Chapter Outline

I. Computer Crime and the Internet
  1. Computer Crime – Any wrongful act that is directed against computers and computer parts or that involves wrongful use of abuse of computers or software
  2. Three categories:
    a. The computer is the object of a crime
    b. The computer is the subject of a crime
    c. The computer is the instrument of a crime
  A. Cyber Crime
    a. A crime that occurs online, in the virtual community of the Internet, as opposed to in the physical world
  B. Opportunity and Anonymity
II. Cyber Crimes against Persons and Property
  A. Cyber Consumer Fraud
    a. Cyber fraud – any misrepresentation knowingly made over the Internet with the intention of deceiving another and on which a reasonable person would and does rely to his or her detriment
    1. Online Retail Fraud
    2. Online Auction Fraud
  B. Cyber Theft
    1. Identity Theft – the theft of personal information, such as a person's name, driver's license number, or Social Security Number
    2. Phishing – perpetrators "fish" for financial data and passwords from consumers by posing as a legitimate business
  C. Cyber Aggression and the New Media
    1. Cyberstalking

266

            a. The crime of stalking, committed in cyberspace through the use of
               the Internet, e-mail, or another form of electronic communication
      2. Cyberbullying
            a. Willful and repeated emotional harm inflicted through the use of
               electronic devices such as computers and cell phones
III. Cyber Crimes in the Business World
   A. Credit-Card Crime on the Web
   B. Hackers
            a. Hacker – a person who uses one computer to break into another
            b. Botnet – a network of computers that have been appropriated
               without the knowledge of their owners and used to spread harmful
               programs via the Internet
      1. Malware – programs that are harmful to computers
            a. Worm – software program that is capable of reproducing itself as it
               spreads
            b. Virus – software program that must be attached to an infested host
               file to travel from one computer network to another
      2. The Scope of the Problem
      3. Cyberwarfare
            a. Denial of Service Attacks – an attack on a computer system or
               Web site that results in a severe degradation of the service being
               offered
   C. The Spread of Spam
   D. Pirating Intellectual Property Online
   E. Electronic Banking and Money Laundering
      1. Cleaning Dirty Money
            a. Money laundering – the introduction of illegally gained funds into
               the legal financial system with the goal of covering up the funds'
               true origin
      2. Digital Currency
IV. Cyber Crimes Against the Community
   A. Online Pornography
      1. Internet is conducive to child pornography for a number of reasons:
            a. Speed
            b. Security
            c. Anonymity
   B. Gambling in Cyberspace
V. Fighting Cyber Crime
   A. On the Cyber Beat: Challenges for Law Enforcement
      1. Cyber Forensics – the application of computer technology to finding
         and utilizing evidence of cyber crimes
            a. Main goal of cyber forensics is to gather digital evidence
                i. Digital evidence – information or data of value to a criminal
                   investigation that is either stored or transmitted by electronic
                   means

267

    2. Jurisdictional Challenges
        a. Domestic Jurisdiction
        b. International Jurisdiction
    B. Federal Law Enforcement and Cyber Crime
        1. The Federal Bureau of Investigation
        2. The United States Secret Service
    C. Private Efforts to Combat Cyber Crime
        1. The Conficker Scare
        2. Encryption – the process by which a message is transmitted into a form or code that the sender and receiver intend not to be understandable by third parties
VI. Freedom of Speech on the Internet
    A. Hate Speech on the Internet
        a. Hate speech – speech that is intended to offend an individual on the basis of her or his race, gender, religion, sexual orientation, ethnicity, or disability
        1. The Supreme Court and Hate Speech
        2. Questions of Regulation
    B. Obscenity on the Internet
        1. Obscenity – speech that is not protected by the First Amendment because it is deemed to be offensive to community standards of decency
VII. Criminal Justice: Looking to the Future
    A. Trends for the Future
        1. Changing demographics
        2. Technological advances
        3. Increasing diversity
        4. Globalization of crime
VIII. Criminal Justice in Action: Virtual Child Pornography

Key Terms

Botnet (pg. 639)
Computer crime (pg. 633)
Computer forensics (pg. 646)
Cyber crime (pg. 633)
Cyberbullying 9pg. 637)
Cyber fraud (pg. 635)
Cyberstalking (pg. 637)
Digital Evidence (pg. 646)
Denial of service attack (pg. 640)
Encryption (pg. 650)
Hacker (pg. 638)
Hate speech (pg. 651)

Special Projects

1. Using popular media, research an incident where a computer was hacked or attacked by a worm or virus. Identify (1) the type of cyber crime involved in the incident, (2) the source of the attack, if known, (3) the victim, and (4) the consequences or resulting damage. With regard to your own personal computer, identify the steps that you have taken to protect it from a similar attack.

2. Look at a large scale retail or Internet auction site (e.g., major retailer, eBay etc...) and locate their user policies including policies related to fraud and criminal activity. What protections has the retailer (commercial business) put in place to thwart hacking and frauds? Would you (as a consumer) feel safe shopping or using their website? Print the policies directly from the website. Prepare a one page report on what you learned and attach the retailer policies to your report.

3. Suppose you were the victim of identity theft stemming from a purchase you made online. What steps would (should you) take to address the crime and protect yourself in the future? Who would you report the crime to? Lastly, visit the credit reporting agency websites. Do they offer additional information for consumer protection? Be prepared to report your research and findings to the class.

Practice Test

True-False

_____1.   The challenge for law enforcement is to apply traditional laws to crimes committed in the new frontier of "cyber space."

_____2.   Most cyber crimes are not new; they are existing crimes in which the Internet is the instrument of wrongdoing.

_____3.   Online auction fraud occurs when a consumer makes the auction purchase but does not receive the item (it is never delivered).

_____4. Phishing is a form of hacking.

_____5. It is a violation of the First Amendment to use the Internet (such as host a website) to advocate violence against African Americans, Jewish people, homosexuals, or any other group.

_____6. Worms and viruses can make the Internet a dangerous place for businesses and consumers.

_____7. Cyberwarfare is an attack on terrorist Web sites.

_____8. Emails are considered to be intellectual property.

_____9. The Internet is conducive to crime because it provides users with an opportunity to remain anonymous during communication.

_____10. Cyberbullying is essentially kids being mean to other kids in a willful manner.

Multiple Choice

1. In 2008, of total complaints received, what percentage of complaints came into the Internet Crime Complaint Center for online auction fraud?
　　a. 9%
　　b. 18%
　　c. 22%
　　d. 26%

2. In 2008, of total complaints received, what percentage of complaints came into the Internet Crime Complaint Center for online identity theft?
　　a. 3%
　　b. 14%
　　c. 17%
　　d. 23%

3. In order to protect yourself from identity theft, the text suggests all of the following EXCEPT:
　　a. shredding all non-essential material containing personal identity information.
　　b. securing personal information that is stored on your computer.
　　c. restricting Internet use to websites that only have the domains ".org" or ".gov".
　　d. not carrying unnecessary identification in a wallet.

4. Which of the following is a form of identity theft?
    a. Using digital currency
    b. Software piracy
    c. Hacking
    d. Phishing

5. According to the text and in the context of computers, the legal term for "kids being mean to each other" is
    a. hate speech.
    b. cyberbullying.
    c. cyberstalking.
    d. obscenity.

6. Which one is not identified in the text as "malware"?
    a. Virus
    b. Botnet
    c. Worm
    d. Phishing

7. What is the significance of the United States Supreme Court ruling in *MGM Studios v. Grokster*?
    a. The case provided for a more even distribution of royalties among stakeholders.
    b. The case provided the film and music industry with the ability to file lawsuits against Internet file-sharing websites that market software designed to illegally download intellectual property.
    c. The case restricted the sales on online "mp3" files and "e-books" to only those retailers who are authorized by the production house.
    d. The case allowed the music and film industry to deploy software to track oversees film and music sales—this provided the industries the ability to recover royalties that to date had gone unpaid because of international law.

8. According to the text, one drawback of encryption technology is that it
    a. becomes obsolete at a rapid pace.
    b. is hard for the average person to use.
    c. makes it hard for the user to read plaintext .
    d. is only available for pc based systems.

9. Cyberbullying occurs when
    a. a person inadvertently views offensive material online.
    b. a person inadvertently sends an unintended recipient an e-mail.
    c. a person uses a computer or electronic device to inflict willful and repeated emotional harm.
    d. a person sends pornographic material over the Internet and the recipient is not at least 18 years of age.

271

10. According to the text: speed, security, and anonymity are three characteristics that make the Internet conducive to
     a. child pornography.
     b. online obscenity.
     c. online shopping.
     d. online social networking.

11. Radio Frequency Identification (RFID) has application in both the commercial business and law enforcement fields. Law enforcement often utilizes it to track down and locate offenders (i.e., embedded in passports, credit cards). This technology utilizes personal data---therefore its very nature leaves it vulnerable to criminal activity such as identity theft by
     a. phishing.
     b. hacking.
     c. encryption.
     d. data mining.

12. Which one is NOT considered to be vulnerable to piracy?
     a. Books
     b. Films
     c. E-mails
     d. Software

13. With regard to the Internet and free speech; which speech is NOT protected?
     a. Religious speech
     b. Hate speech
     c. Obscenity
     d. Political speech

14. With regard to free speech; speech loses its protection when the speaker
     a. is a member of a terrorist group.
     b. supports religious extremism.
     c. intends to inflict punishment, loss or pain on another through the commission of an unlawful act.
     d. advocates the unlawful behavior of activist groups such as eco-terrorists.

15. Which one is NOT considered to be a "test" to determine if material is obscene?
     a. The average person would find the material causes lascivious or lustful thoughts and desires.
     b. The material is viewed to be obscene by spiritual leaders.
     c. The material describes, in an offensive way, sexual conduct as defined by state law.
     d. The material lacks serious literary, artistic, political or scientific value.

272

16. Many experts believe that the number of Internet-enabled crimes will increase. Which one does NOT support this statement?
  a. The male population surge will result in more computer programmers and by default more hackers
  b. As the price of technology drops more people will plug in
  c. As the price of technology drops, computers will play a larger role in daily life
  d. The growth of e-commerce has resulted in a business model that businesses have come to rely on

17. Approximately how many Americans are affected by cyberstalking each year?
  a. Just under 1 million
  b. Just over 1 million
  c. 2.8 million
  d. 3.4 million

18. When a criminal sends a fraudulent e-mail to a consumer, prompting the consumer to enter personal identification information about themselves (e.g., passwords, birth date), is best described as
  a. hacking.
  b. surfing.
  c. encrypting.
  d. phishing.

19. Introducing illegally gained funds into the legal financial system is with the intended goal of covering up the source of those funds is known as
  a. digital currency.
  b. piracy.
  c. laundering.
  d. encoding.

20. Which one is NOT a government sanctioned measure of protection for intellectual property?
  a. Copyright
  b. U.S. law
  c. Patent
  d. CAN-SPAM Act

21. According to the text, the context of crime fighting over the next few decades will undoubtedly be influenced by all of the following EXCEPT:
  a. DNA fingerprinting
  b. a more diverse group of law enforcement professionals.
  c. a declining male demographic.
  d. the domestication of crime---crime will stay mostly on U.S. soil.

22. What tool do online retailers and other Web sites use to track consumer behaviors on the Internet?
   a. Cracking
   b. Cookies
   c. Botnets
   d. Piracy

Fill in the Blank

1. _____ is speech that is NOT protected by the First Amendment.

2. The application of science to find evidence of cyber crimes is known as cyber _____.

3. Books, movies, software, and music are all examples of _____ property.

4. Unsolicited junk email is called _____.

5. A computer program capable of reproducing itself as it spreads from one computer to the next is called a a(n) _____.

6. The process of sending an email that "tricks" a person (consumer) into revealing personal information with the intention of using that person's information to facilitate a future crime is known as _____.

7. A person who uses one computer to break into another computer is called a(n) _____.

8. An act involving the wrongful use or abuse of computers or software is called _____ crime.

9. Stalking is a _____ that puts a person in reasonable fear of personal safety or the safety of the person's immediate family.

10. A misrepresentation made over the Internet with the intent to deceive another reasonable person is called cyber _____.

Short Essays

1. Distinguish cyber crime from traditional crime.

2. Indicate how the Internet has expanded opportunities for identity theft.

3. Explain the differences between cyberstalking and cyberbullying.

4. Describe the following three types of malware (a) botnets, (b) worms, and (c) viruses.

5. Explain how the Internet has contributed to piracy of intellectual property.

7. Indicate how encryption programs protect digital data from unauthorized access.

8. Explain why the right to free speech on the Internet is not absolute.

Answer Key

True-False:
1. T, see pg. 634, LO1
2. T, see pg. 634, LO1
3. F, see pg. 635, LO1
4. F, see pg. 636, LO2
5. F, see pg. 651, LO8
6. T, see pg. 639, LO4
7. F, see pgs. 639-640, LO4
8. F, see pg. 640, LO7
9. T, see pg. 644, LO 1/6
10. T, see pg. 637, LO3

Multiple Choice:
1. d, see pg. 635, LO2
2. a, see pg. 635, LO2
3. c, see pg. 636, LO2
4. d, see pg. 636, LO2
5. b, see pg. 637, LO3
6. d, see pg. 639, LO4
7. b, see pg. 641, LO5
8. a, see pg. 650, LO7
9. c, see pgs. 637-638, LO3
10. a, see pgs. 643-644, LO6
11. b, see pg. 639, LO4
12. c, see pg. 640, LO5
13. c, see pg. 652, LO8
14. c, see pg. 651, LO8
15. b, see pg. 652, LO8
16. a, see pg. 654, LO1
17. d, see pg. 637, LO3
18. d, see pg. 636, LO2/4
19. c, see pg. 642, LO5
20. d, see pg. 640, LO5
21. d, see pg. 655, LO1
22. b, see pg. 636, LO2

Fill in the Blank:
1. obscenity, see pg. 652, LO8
2. forensics, see pg. 646, LO7
3. intellectual, see pg. 640, LO5
4. spam, see pg. 640, LO4/7
5. worm, see pg. 639, LO4
6. phishing, see pg. 636, LO2/4
7. hacker, see pg. 639, LO2/4
8. computer, see pg. 568, LO1
9. credible threat, see pg. 637, LO3
10. fraud, see pg. 635, LO1

Short Essays:
1. See pgs. 633-634, LO1
2. See pg. 636, LO2
3. See pgs. 637-638, LO3
4. See pg. 639, LO4
5. See pgs. 640-641, LO5
6. See pgs. 643-644, LO6
7. See pg. 650, LO7
8. See pg. 652, LO8